USER EDUCATION IN LIBRARIES

Nancy Fjällbrant
and
Malcolm Stevenson

USER EDUCATION IN LIBRARIES

Nancy Fjällbrant
and
Malcolm Stevenson

CLIVE BINGLEY
LONDON

LINNET BOOKS
HAMDEN · CONN

FIRST PUBLISHED 1978 BY CLIVE BINGLEY LTD
16 PEMBRIDGE ROAD LONDON W11 UK
SIMULTANEOUSLY PUBLISHED IN THE USA BY LINNET BOOKS
AN IMPRINT OF THE SHOE STRING PRESS INC
995 SHERMAN AVENUE HAMDEN CONNECTICUT 06514
SET IN 10 ON 11 POINT UNIVERS BY ALLSET
PRINTED IN GREAT BRITAIN BY REDWOOD BURN LTD
TROWBRIDGE AND ESHER
COPYRIGHT © NANCY FJÄLLBRANT
AND MALCOLM STEVENSON
ALL RIGHTS RESERVED
BINGLEY ISBN: 0 85157 251 0
LINNET ISBN: 0 208 01664 3

Library of Congress Cataloging in Publication Data

Fjällbrant, Nancy, 1934-
    User education in libraries.

    Bibliography: p.
    Includes index.
    1. Library orientation.   I. Stevenson, Malcolm
B., joint author.   II. Title.
Z711.2.F58   028.7   77-19192
ISBN 0-208-01664-3 (Linnet)

Contents

Figures in the text

Tables in the text

6

Preface

THE AIM of this book is to provide a practical introduction to the subject of the education of library users. The last five to ten years has seen a considerable growth of interest in the subject and the situation has now been reached where many are questioning the methods adopted in the past. Gordon Wright's book *The library in colleges of commerce and technology—a guide to the use of a library as instrument of education* published in 1966 was the forerunner. It was followed by Hazel Mews' invaluable handbook *Reader instruction in colleges and universities*. These were both practical books using case studies to illustrate the subject. It is hoped that this book will also help people involved in user education by means of up-to-date examples of, and the thinking behind, user education programmes. Three case studies of different approaches to user education are presented—the person-to-person approach (University of Sussex, England), the systematic approach (Chalmers University of Technology, Gothenburg, Sweden), and the project-orientated approach (Roskilde University Centre, Denmark). Surveys are given of the present state of the art of user education in the United Kingdom, Scandinavia and the USA.

Much of the material in chapters two, three, five, and twelve has previously appeared in the following journal articles: 'Planning a programme of library user education' *Journal of librarianship* 9 (3) 1977; 'Teaching methods for the education of the library user' *Libri* 26 (4) 1976; 'Evaluation in a user education programme' *Journal of librarianship* 9 (2) 1977; and 'User education and its integration into the functioning of the academic library' *Nordisk Tidskrift för Bok-och Biblioteksväsen* 64 1977. Similarly, much of the descriptive material in chapter nine is taken from BLRD Report number 5320 *User education programmes: a study of their development, organisation, methods and assessment*, 1977. The authors would like to express their grateful thanks for permission to make use of this material. They would also like to thank the project team at Roskilde University Centre—Tamar Bermann, Birgitte Lau, Karen Risager and Niels Erik Wille—for permission to use their report 'Library user education in the framework of project studies: teaching humanities students literature searching during their basic studies programme at Roskilde University Centre' in the writing of chapter eight.

The authors would like to thank Vera From, Moira Halloways and Kerstin McCarthy, for patient and persistent help with the manuscript production and proofreading, Mr Dennis Cox, Librarian of Leeds University, Mr Peter Lewis, Librarian of Sussex University, and Dr Sven Westberg, the Library Director of Chalmers University of Technology, Gothenburg, for their continuous help and encouragement.

CHAPTER ONE

User education—an introduction

THE HISTORY of the development of user education as it applies in libraries is well documented. Bonn's definitive history of the whole field which appeared in 1960 was updated by Tidmarsh who concentrated on instruction in the use of academic libraries. She also described developments in the United Kingdom in the theory and practice of user education following the proposals for a three-stage programme put forward in 1949 by the British Library Association University and Research Section. The coverage of the British scene was further developed for the period 1966-1970 by Mews who examined courses reported during that period, particularly those involving instruction for new students and undergraduates. In America, the approaches to teaching library skills to college students have been studied by Dudley. More recently Givens has studied the libraries' response to the educational developments of the 'sixties. In addition to these descriptive reviews bibliographies have been compiled by Mirwis, covering academic library instruction in the USA in the period 1960-1970, and by Crossley and Clews, whose bibliography was compiled for a literature review on the evaluation of the use of educational technology in information handling instruction. Orientation and instructional programmes have been surveyed in the USA, by Melum, Griffin and Clarke and, in the UK, by Fox.

There have been many seminars and conferences on the theme in recent years at both national and international levels. One such workshop in the UK held in 1973 and supported by OSTI (now British Library Research and Development Department) concluded that research or investigation was required into thirteen areas of the user education field. The outcome of some of those investigations is discussed in chapter nine. Papers presented at American conferences on library orientation and instruction have been collected together in a series produced by Pierian Press. A collection of papers on the theme has been brought together by Lubans in *Educating the library user* and two issues of *Drexel Library quarterly* have been devoted to library instruction.

An introductory handbook for those involved in user education was prepared by Mews, based on her teaching experiences at the University of Reading. Considerable use was made of case histories in this book as it was in an earlier introductory handbook by Wright on the use of a library as an instrument of education.

The considerable amount of writing on the theme of user education, only superficially covered above, shows clearly the amount of interest in the subject. That user education has so developed and been accepted by librarians as an integral part of their function poses the question— Why? What are the needs seen by librarians that have led to the wide acceptance of the belief in the value of user education?

The traditional view

Early attempts to explain why user education was necessary were based mainly on the belief that to know how to use a library was an essential part of the education-for-life process, to prepare the student for the continuing process of self-education once the formal process had been completed. In 1926 Cuming expressed the view that to learn how to use a library and to acquire a disinterested love of reading are important elements of education. To a certain extent this is still true. The explosion of knowledge places greater stress on the ability to continue to learn throughout life. A student in higher education may have developed a logical, creative and critical approach to his subject but he may not have been taught independence. For example, his reading lists may have been pre-selected for him. To be independent the student needs the knowledge and skill to find his own way.

Not only in principle but also in practice can it be shown that user education is necessary. The Parry Report of 1967 contained a survey of undergraduate use of libraries which showed that only 37% of students claimed to know what abstract journals were and that 22% claimed not to know whether the library had an author catalogue or not, and 28% whether it had a subject catalogue or not. One would hope that with the increase in the past ten years of user education programmes these figures would have by now changed for the better. However it would be a brave person who claimed all was now well. At a practical level several changes over the past few years have, if anything, pointed to a greater need for helping the user. The emphasis on self-education has led to the increased use of tutorials, seminars, projects, and guided reading as teaching methods, and less reliance on formal lectures. There is an implicit assumption in this educational change that the learner is capable of finding material relevant to his needs. In practice such an assumption is not valid; the learner requires to be taught that capability. Only then is he able to prepare himself to take a full and active part in such learning methods.

Another factor pointing to the need for instruction is the growth in the number of interdisciplinary courses. Such courses which cut across the traditional boundaries of subjects have been a particular feature of the new universities and polytechnics and are becoming increasingly important in all institutions of higher education. These courses bring with them greater problems for the student in the location and organisation of material for study. The quantity of material to be searched because of the diverse disciplines involved requires that the student should be helped to find his way. It is not just the quantity of the material which makes help essential but also the diversity of the sources and formats. Without help the student could never make efficient use of all the material that is available and useful to him.

Just as principles and practicalities contribute to the justification of user education so too does the philosophy of active librarianship propounded by Palmer who claims that as a profession we must stop hoarding our bibliographic knowledge and concealing our awareness of the problems of information retrieval. We must stop waiting to be asked to share this special knowledge. We must insist upon making it available to all users, in every conceivable form and at every accessible point of need. Then and only then, can we claim to be complete librarians.

An alternative view

Though the reasons expressed above have considerable validity in establishing the reason why user education programmes have proliferated they can be seen to be the librarian's expression of a justification for involvement in user education. The librarian's concept of what the need is, is not always at one with that of the user. Many users would argue that there is a communications barrier between the librarian and the user. Much library instruction is only rendered necessary by the complexity and inefficiency of the systems employed by librarians. The first task of any user education programme should be to ensure that the systems are effective, straightforward and self-explanatory. Too much time and effort is wasted explaining away the problems of the librarian's own making, the professional mysteries; time and effort that could more valuably be spent making libraries easier to use.

What are these barriers to communication erected by librarians between themselves and their users? Library buildings are not always the easiest of places to understand and find one's way around. Though this may be a legacy of a previous era as far as the physical structure of the building is concerned, there are few excuses for inadequate guiding and signposting of the building. Some librarians feel that the only reason they need to provide orientation tours is to make up for inadequate guiding. Information should be available to the user at the point of need or as C E N Childs, Librarian of Brunel University, puts it—if all the library staff were propped up dead at their posts . . . it should still be possible for a student on his first visit to the library to

11

find his way to the books he needs. Too often though what guiding is provided is designed by librarians with librarians in mind. Very few libraries employ professional design help, though this situation is now changing rapidly.

Within the library building there is another barrier to communication. The catalogue, the so-called key to finding required material within the library, is often incomprehensible to the user. Cataloguing is one of the mystiques of the profession and has been developed almost into an art for its own sake. Whilst within the academic community there are some who will benefit from the use of a fully developed catalogue, the great majority of users require a simple finding list—a true key to locating required material—with a simple subject index that uses a language and terminology they understand. Attempts by librarians, usually in written form, to explain the use of the catalogue, introduce the user to yet another barrier to ease of use of the library. Such productions inevitably use a discipline-orientated terminology — jargon. This slips all too easily into publications, into talks, into audio-visual programmes, and only serves to perpetuate the mystique of the profession.

In many instances there are also physical barriers to be overcome. The library may have problems of heating and noise control. It may have inadequate borrowing and opening hours or a shortage of required books. Complexities of use and inefficiencies of the systems employed create attitudes in the users which affect the atmosphere in which user education programmes have to operate. Every effort should be made initially to minimise situations likely to create unhelpful attitudes and thus to create a climate in which user education can succeed. As Line puts it, the aim should be to orientate all the library's processes and services towards user needs so that, for example, the catalogues are readily usable in addition (if necessary in preference) to being biblio-graphically accurate. The amount of use of a library is not a true measure of success; the usability of the whole library is. Unfortunately, according to Thornton, libraries employing simple methods of book arrangement, basic information only on catalogue cards, and simple shelf arrangements are looked upon as 'out-of-date' by so-called pro-gressive libraries. Thornton's idea of a library is one in which readers are helped to help themselves, are encouraged to browse and can find their own way around.

What then is user education concerned with? In her book on reader instruction Mews defines that topic as instruction given to readers to help them make the best use of a library. A workshop on the subject at Bath sponsored by OSTI suggested that the purpose of user education was not solely to stimulate library use since other sources of informa-tion are equally important. This idea parallels the thoughts of Gordon

Wright in an earlier book on library instruction. He suggested that the student cannot be taught the use of the library in splendid isolation, but must see it as a continuous process of education in which the varied facets of communication are inextricably intermixed. If user education is to be involved with the whole information/communication process, then on the narrower level it must be concerned with the total inter-action of the user with the library. Every contact with the library, formal or informal, involving contact with library staff or not, will have an educational value. User education in library terms should therefore be aimed at maximising that value. If this is the case then user education cannot be seen as a peripheral activity of the library; it is central to its whole purpose.

It is unfortunate therefore that traditional methods of user education do not emphasise this important role. The pattern of many user education programmes is usually very similar to that proposed at the Royal Society Scientific Information Conference in 1948 and by the Library Association University and Research Section one year later, namely one of courses given to new students to introduce them to library use, and to advanced students on the structure of the literature of given subject fields. The approach is naturally disjointed being concentrated on particular periods of time when courses are given; at other times little activity is apparent. It can be represented graphically, as shown in figure one.

This pattern may be a continuing programme, each stage building on the last, but it is not continuous. It cannot lead to real integration of courses with departmental teaching. It can also tend to relegate the daily more informal contact and communication between librarian and user. In addition, the two components, orientation and instruction, in a more idealistic approach would not be separable. Elements of each are important in the interaction of the user with the library—orientation more so in the first few months, instruction as the student's course develops—but at all times both elements of help are available. Such a model of user education as is shown in figure two does not preclude the holding of organised courses of lectures or seminars at appropriate points in the student's course, but what it does do is to bring within the ambit of consideration as user education all other forms of interaction, even on a daily basis, of the user and the library.

The two elements making up this ideal picture can be defined as follows. Orientation is primarily concerned with ways of introducing the user to the general techniques of library usage and services available in libraries and, in particular to the organisation, services and layout of one particular library; bibliographical instruction is the introduction to the user of the information resources available in particular subject disciplines and the techniques of making use of those resources. There is a body of thought which considers that orientation is not only concerned with cognitive objectives aimed at introducing such factual information, but also with affective objectives. These might be aimed at creating the right kind of atmosphere for effective communication between user and librarian, at creating certain attitudes towards libraries on the part of the user and presenting an image of libraries as helpful, friendly institutions. The end product of the orientation process, according to Jolley, should be a student confident that the library staff is competent and willing to help him, and able to seek such help with complete absence of self-consciousness or diffidence. The implications of this for the librarian are discussed in chapter thirteen. User education is thus directed to specific individual users and expectations, not to some mythical homogeneous student type. The two major conclusions of Melum's survey were that library instruction is effective only at a time of need and that learning to use a library is a continuous process. A possible pattern to achieve this might be devised along the lines of the ideal model in figure two—ie provision of a continuing programme of user education on a person-to-person basis, available at the time of need. A faltering attempt to match this ideal is described in chapter six.

That an ideal situation has not been achieved is hardly surprising when one considers the problems faced in operating a more traditional approach to user education. At a practical level these relate to the organisation of courses—timing, timetabling, size of group, optimum length, etc—as well as the content of the course itself. These have been fully discussed by Mews and Scrivener among others. Also at a practical level, the basic lack of guiding in libraries has been mentioned as has the prevalence of jargon which not only perpetuates the mysteries of librarianship but also does little to create a good image of the librarian. This apparent lack of a positive image is in itself a practical barrier to the establishment of effective user education. However even a positive image is not necessarily a key to success. It is not enough for the student to be stimulated by the librarian to make use of the library. His teachers must provide him with experiences convincing him that using the library is a necessary and meaningful part of education. This attitude of the teaching staff probably provides the greatest problem for the advancement and development of user education. The solution seen by librarians to this problem is to integrate more closely the user education programme with the academic teaching programme, involving the closer cooperation of librarian with teaching faculty, lecturers and librarians working together in the development of lecture courses so that all the resources of the library can be brought in to improve the quality of the education given to students. The immediate outcome of this closer

14

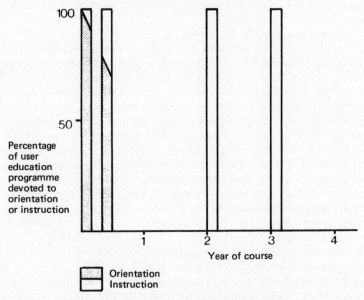

Figure 1: The usual pattern of user education

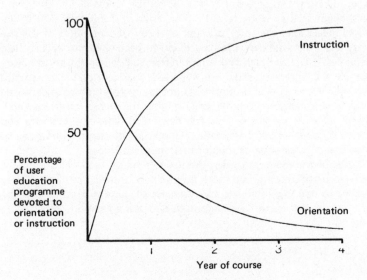

Figure 2: User education—an ideal

cooperation is a greater and more relevant use of practical work included in user education programmes.

However cooperation on an ongoing basis is required as students are continually faced with problems for solution. Hopefully this will lead to teachers and librarians working together in the development of lecture courses so that library resources can be used to the full. This would involve the incorporation of objectives of user education in the formulation of overall objectives for the academic course, and the cooperative development of instructional methods to see that those objectives are attained. Such cooperation is beginning to occur in the UK with the inclusion in several CNAA degree submissions of user education as an integral component. Alternative forms of user education have been suggested along the lines of this ideal librarian/faculty cooperation. They tend to rely on a change in the university teaching pattern to take more account of the library. In particular, mention must be made of the concept of the library college, the key to which according to Shores is a college in which the student's dominant learning mode is independent study in the library, bibliographically guided, intellectually aroused, and spiritually stirred by the faculty. This idea of making teaching library—rather than lecture—orientated was the basis of the well-known Monteith College experiment. Such a concept is the ultimate step in the integration of user education into the academic curriculum.

An alternative approach, getting away from formal methods, is described by Hatt who argues that it is 'better for people to find things out for themselves than to be taught'. The move from the formal to the informal means that the tutor is better able to meet the needs of the students and in the process they are likely to become better able to help themselves. Greater planning is required in such an approach to ensure that all the necessary skills are imparted. In considering alternative methods of user education one must not lose sight of more fundamental ideals. Hackman, for example, predicts that the revolution in user education, when it comes, will be less concerned with new methods and more with a realistic and emphatic relationship between the librarian and student and a clearer perception of their mutual purpose.

Some of the more important problems faced by user education in its many formats are discussed more fully in the following chapters. They are highlighted by reference to overviews of current practice and the descriptions of three different approaches to user education.

CHAPTER TWO

The definition of goals and objectives
for a programme of user education

IN PLANNING education programmes for library users, it is necessary to define the main goals and specific objectives for the courses to be given, the course-content and timing of the various stages, and the teaching methods and media to be used. The result of this planning is then tested in a practical situation, and evaluation is carried out in order to assess the effectiveness of the programme. The development of a course of education is represented diagramatically in figure three. This chapter will describe the initial planning of a course of user education—the definition of goals and objectives. The timing of the various stages, the teaching methods and media to be used will be discussed in chapter three, and chapter five will provide an introduction to evaluation of library user education programmes.

The formulation of goals and objectives

Education is often regarded as a process which changes the learners—a process 'in which someone has to decide what changes are possible and desirable. Every teacher-student interaction is based on some implicit conviction on the part of both teacher and student about the possibility and desirability of certain changes' (Bloom et al, 1971).

The planning of a programme of education often begins with the verbal formulation of the possible and desirable changes in a so-called statement of goals and objectives. (The term 'goal' will be used to express broad, general statements of purpose, whereas 'objective' will be used to express specific short-term aims, in agreement with the main goals.) The verbal formulation of goals and objectives does not, however, ensure that the goals expressed are the same as the implicit goals. It should also be realised that changes can occur which have not been foreseen; some of these may be desirable, others may be undesirable. In addition, students will not all change to the same extent, or even in the same way.

The clear definition of the changes desired, as a result of a given educational process, in a statement of goals and objectives, facilitates the choice of course content and of media and methods for presenting this material, and the timing of the different parts. At the same time it provides a focal

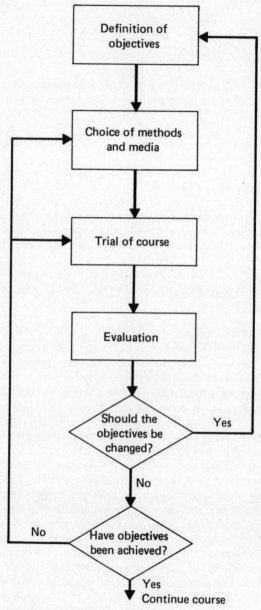

Figure 3: Development of a course of education

point for evaluation, which is concerned, in part, with relating changes in a student's behaviour to the purposes of the educational programme.

Goals and objectives can be divided, for purposes of convenience, into three main groups—cognitive, affective and psychomotor. In library user education, the objectives are to be found mainly in the cognitive and affective domains.

Cognitive goals and objectives are concerned with understanding various concepts. Within the cognitive domain the goals and objectives can be arranged according to degree of complexity—from complex to simple and from abstract to concrete. An attempt to provide a framework for the range of cognitive objectives has been developed by, amongst others, Bloom (1956). This is known as the 'Taxonomy of educational objectives'—a hierarchical classification scheme for cognitive objectives—the lowest level of the hierarchy corresponding to the least complex objectives, increasing complexity being represented at higher levels in the hierarchical structure.

Affective goals and objectives are concerned with feelings—such as whether the student wants to, and subsequently does, behave in various educationally desirable ways, as for example the pleasure involved in making use of library resources in order to find information. These affective goals and objectives are of considerable long-term importance for the behaviour of the student. An attempt has also been made to provide a framework for affective goals and objectives (Krathwohl et al, 1964).

There is usually a close inter-relationship between cognitive and affective objectives. The verbally expressed goals and objectives for a given course of instruction tend to describe cognitive elements. There are however, in many cases, affective components, implicit in these statements. Most teachers hope that their students will develop a continuing positive interest in the material being taught; but these goals are often unspecified in a statement of objectives.

Thus in library user instruction in the cognitive domain the student should know how to make use of specific library tools such as catalogues and abstracts when asked to do so. In the affective domain the student will make use of these resources, when appropriate in connection with his information needs, after he has learnt how to use them.

Goals and objectives should be based on the views of the people participating in the various educational processes. 'There is no doubt that the student must be involved in the process of decision about educational goals and objectives . . . At the very least, it is to be desired that the learner accept the goals. At the other extreme it is to be desired that he has some sense of participation in setting them. However, we would argue that the full responsibility for setting goals cannot be placed on the student, who in most cases will not be able to foresee the alternatives available and in many cases cannot fully appreciate the implications of particular choices' (Bloom et al, 1971).

Goals and objectives for library user education

In considering the goals and objectives for library user education, one becomes aware that, if expressed at all, these tend to be very vague. Thus Lubans, in 1974, said that 'several locally developed guidelines for instruction in library skills have been drawn up' but that 'these guidelines are rarely based on specific objectives'. Similarly, Stevenson has made the statement that 'few librarians have expressed either the aims or objectives for reader instruction'.

The goals and objectives for programmes of library user education must be in agreement with the general aims of the university library; these aims must, in turn, be related to the goals and aims of higher education. The general goals of a university library may be expressed in the following way:

1 To contribute to the realisation of the aims of the university, with regard to teaching, learning and research, by acquisition of printed and non-print material necessary to cover present day and future information needs.

2 To register and store the material acquired in such a way that it not only permits, but even actively stimulates the use of this material.

3 To adapt these information resources and services to the changing needs of the university and society.

4 To contribute to the integration of both national and international information resources within the university.

One way of stimulating the active use of the information stored in the library is by teaching the library user how to obtain information from the material available. Thus a general goal for a programme of user education for any type of library, is likely to include an attempt to create an awareness of the resources available. In special libraries, for such subjects as science, medicine, or technology, where the rate of growth of literature is rapid, the need for user instruction is particularly marked.

The need for cooperation between library staff, academic staff and students, in the formulation of goals and objectives for library education

Library use is not part of a separate academic discipline such as zoology, history, or sociology. It consists of a series of skills which can be made use of in connection with different academic studies. This would suggest that education in library use should be closely integrated with the teaching programmes within the various academic disciplines. As the type of literature and the information sources vary widely between different areas of study, such as, for example, the natural sciences and the liberal arts, one would expect that the specific objectives for library instruction in these disciplines would show differences whereas the main goals might well be similar.

Several investigators have pointed out the need for cooperation between library and academic staff. For example, Knapp states that (competence in use of the library) 'should be integrated into the total curriculum. But it cannot be so integrated until the faculty as a whole is ready to recognise the validity of its claim and to implement this recognition through regularly established procedures of curriculum development.' Similarly, Mackenzie points out that 'the department view of what is required will often conflict with the library's.' He suggests that both sides should cooperate in the teaching and gradually learn from each other. Lubans suggests the problem-solving approach— as a solution for limiting non-use it is recommended that faculty involve the use of literature in research or problem solving assignments whenever possible (Lubans, 1971).

The need for cooperation between library staff, academic staff, and students can be represented as in figure four. Vogel posed the following questions:

1 Do librarians know what the student perceives about the services in the library?

2 Do librarians know what the student really needs to know (or perceives necessary to know) about the library?

3 Do librarians know whom the student is most likely to approach if he has informational needs?

In other words, does a basic conflict of attitudes and interests exist between students and librarians?

Goals and objectives for educational programmes are often perceived differently by different groups of people concerned with the instruction. Thus, in university courses, the academic staff may be aiming to teach broad general concepts within a specific discipline, whereas the students taking part in the instruction may be aiming to pass a given examination as quickly as possible in order to obtain a degree. With regard to university library education there is, in addition to the academic staff and the students, a third group concerned with user education—the library staff. The goals and objectives perceived by these three groups will differ. Even within each of the groups it is possible to have a wide range of goals and objectives. For example, the library administrative staff might be concerned with the efficient utilisation of the library resources available and consider this to be the main goal of library instruction.

21

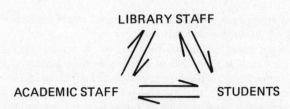

LIBRARY STAFF

ACADEMIC STAFF   STUDENTS

*Figure 4: The relationship between library staff, academic staff,
and students in user education*

Other members might have quite different conceptions of a programme
of user instruction—seeing as an important result a reduction in the
number of 'errors' made by students in requesting material, for example,
thereby speeding up the supply of the material desired.

A pilot study of the needs of the library user, as seen by academic
staff, library staff and students has been carried out, as part of an OSTI
research project, at the Institute for Educational Technology, University
of Surrey, England. In this descriptive study, Roy showed that the
students viewed the library as a tool to be used in response to stimuli
such as essays, projects and exams, whereas the idea of 'most of the
academic staff and all library staff' was that the library should be 'the
centre for information, sources of constant references and stimulus to
the course'.

A study has also been carried out at Chalmers University of Technology Library, Gothenburg, on the needs of users as perceived by students,
academic staff, library staff, administrative staff, and industrial engineers
and librarians in industrial concerns. The results of this study are
presented in table one.

As can be seen, there were considerable differences between perceived
needs for the use of the library and therefore, the need for library education, as observed by the different groups.

Academic staff and students regarded the library as a source of information for students. The main goal for a programme of user education was considered to be to enable the students to find information on
various topics in connection with their academic studies. Academic
staff stressed the students' need to obtain information as an aid to
independent thinking and problem-solving activities. Students wished to
be able to find information that would be useful for their actual study
projects.

Librarians, on the other hand, were concerned with the utilisation
of resources possessed by the library and the use of specific library
tools such as the card catalogue. Emphasis was on the use of specific

22

GROUP	THEORY	PRACTICE
Undergraduates	Not much reason to use library in first two years. Library—useful as source of material for study projects: literature seminars & undergraduate projects.	Little use of library for optional studies or borrowing. Unaware of tools for information retrieval. Library used in connection with study projects.
Postgraduates	Have experienced problems of information retrieval. Interested in learning how to carry out information searches.	Make greater use of library than undergraduates. More aware of tools for information retrieval.
Academic staff	Student use of library 'desirable' as source of information. Prepared to encourage library use (but not at expense of own courses).	Few teachers actively promote the use of the library in connection with studies. Lack of time for additional material.
Library staff	Library information resources should be of great value for the students. Student should learn how to use the tools at the library.	Lack of contact with academic staff. Difficulties in knowing what courses are planned & therefore what information students are likely to require.
Administrative staff	Library resources should be maximally utilised.	No money provided for instruction in how to use. (This changed to— money provided for instruction).
Industrial engineers & librarians in industrial concerns	Library and instruction in use should be project-linked.	(Use library in connection with industrial projects themselves).

Table 1: Needs of library users as perceived by different groups

tools, rather than on the method of information retrieval in the context of the communication pattern or in connection with the academic courses.

In connection with descriptive observations and interviews carried out as part of the evaluation of introductory courses in information retrieval at Chalmers Library, students described their initial reaction to the library (S = student, I = interviewer):

S: So you come into the library and it's like a jungle, lots of books and so many of them in English.

The jungle parallel seemed popular, as can be seen from another interview:

S: Well you can say that when we came here, one hadn't a clue about how to start, knew nothing, like a jungle. Now we've only just got a little view into the jungle, I mean we couldn't do a really comprehensive search . . . but we can at least make a start.

Students thought that an early introduction course would have been useful:

S: The fear, if you know what I mean, of going into the library would be reduced.
   Yes, that's right, I didn't dare go in there to borrow a book.
I: You mean you really didn't dare to go in to borrow a book?
S: Well you know what I mean, one didn't want to try these things, because, well you'd heard that it was such a difficult business to borrow a book there, so one tried to avoid it as long as possible and borrowed books from the public library instead.

Some of the students interviewed had tried to carry out literature searches prior to taking part in the introductory course in information retrieval. Their experiences can be illustrated by the following interviews.

One student said that he had visited the library a month previous to the course and tried a search on his own:

S: I didn't get anywhere.
I: You didn't get anywhere? What did you do then?
S: First I came in there and saw some books, and I thought they don't have many books. Then I found out that they were just a lot of lists that you could use to look up books. Then somebody helped me, so I found a book and I went home and read it.
I: Did you ask at the information desk?
S: Mm, and she helped me to find a book.
I: Just one book?
S: Well she looked in a card catalogue, and then I looked there.
I: Was it the subject catalogue?
S: Yes that's right.

24

I: Didn't you borrow any more books?
S: No, it seemed so meaningless.

Another of the students had actually carried out a literature search in connection with a tutorial in transportation and logistics, he described how he used the library then:

S: Well, one went about and felt a bit lost at first. Then I asked for help and came to the card catalogues and looked in them and found a few books. But it was . . . well, I got a bit out of it, but not so much really.

These interviews illustrate that students often experience difficulties in their attempts to use academic libraries. Previous experience is based on the use of school libraries and public libraries. The interviews given were typical of students at Chalmers University and they indicate the need for some form of early library orientation and a systematic instruction in the obtaining of information. Studies on perceived needs of library users have been carried out in the USA by, amongst others, Taylor.

As Lubans states, 'most library instruction is based on what we librarians think library users need to know. It is this educated guesswork or perceived need on which many programmes (tour, orientation lectures, a multitude of multi-media presentations and formal courses in bibliography) have been based. Since we are prompted to action by what we observe to be lacking in the library users at the time of the user's need, our response is apt to be a type of bibliographic first aid' (Lubans, 1974).

The result of this perceived need approach may be that a number of short term objectives, such as the use of specific tools, are included in librarians' programmes of user instruction which neglect the main goals of the user—how to find information as quickly as possible. Use of the material stored in the library is an important way in which scientists can acquire new knowledge. It is, however, only one of many ways. It is important to know when to use the library and when not to use the library. Thus verbal communication, with the possibility of direct feedback, is much faster than printed communication, and many scientists and engineers are particularly interested in obtaining information as quickly as possible.

Possibly some of the problems of the existing courses of library instruction for scientists, medical workers and engineers have been due to the failure to identify with the needs of the user and realise the importance of the time aspect of information retrieval. One reason for this may be that many librarians have little training in scientific subjects. One can become so dominated by the library environment that one tends to forget that there are other ways of obtaining information than by the use of bibliographic abstracts and indexes.

25

Librarians have often assumed the role of designers of courses in user instruction. Bloomfield, in a review on the methods of testing library use competence says that 'in the way we have constructed our tests on library use skills it appears that we librarians have shown a poor understanding of the value of the library to our students.' He goes on to say that 'librarians have exalted the card catalogue as the major source for locating books. The card catalogue is one of the most useful tools we have, but it is certainly not the only one. The emphasis placed on the use of the card catalogue suggests that librarians are convinced that a thorough use of the card catalogue is essential to the efficient use of a library.'

The card catalogue is useful, but its usefulness must be assessed in relation to the information resources to which it gives access. The material registered there is usually larger units—that is, books, theses, textbooks etc. These contain, in the case of science and technology, information considerably removed in time from the actual research work. Thus the card catalogue can be useful for orientation or basic knowledge on a topic, but less useful for obtaining access to information on recent research work. The subject catalogue can be very useful if orientation on a given topic is required, as by undergraduates, or librarians, or by academic staff planning a new course. However, for undergraduates working on research projects and for postgraduates and academic staff engaged on research, there are other tools, such as abstracts and indexes, which play a more important role. This would be true in scientific, engineering, and medical projects, but not necessarily in the liberal arts.

Librarians themselves may find the subject catalogue and encyclopedias of great help for general orientation when faced with an information problem, particularly in science and technology, and may thus overemphasise the value of the card catalogue and of encyclopedias in courses of user instruction. Academic staff and research workers on the other hand, who are seldom in need of orientation within their own particular field of research may regard such instruction as less important than that on how to obtain information from journal articles and reports.

Thus it can be seen that differences in goals and objectives between libraries and users may well lead to emphasis on certain aspects of a subject which one of the groups concerned regards as not very important. This in turn can cause problems of motivation and result in a course which is not particularly successful. It would be possible to set up a series of detailed objectives for a course in library instruction, to let the students participate in the course, and show, by pre- and post-instruction tests that the students had learnt a great deal about the use of libraries. However, if there was poor agreement about the goals and main objectives

26

of such instruction, one would expect to find low attendance of students and a lack of interest among the academic staff—a condition frequently described with regard to programmes of user instruction. In these differences of goals and objectives may well lie the explanation for the relative failure of many courses of library instruction. Such courses have often been received with lukewarm enthusiasm by students and staff.

The goals and objectives for a course of library education must be in accordance with the goals expressed by the students and academic staff. As Watkins points out 'it is now and always will be the classroom and its ideals which, by and large, determine the activity at our loan desk'. In designing a course of library education, it is necessary to see that the goals aimed at really do coincide with those of the users.

Examples of goals and objectives for library user education

One of the first lists of objectives for university library instruction was that drawn up by Hutton at the 1942 Aslib conference.

1 To acquire facility to work easily and familiarly with books in large libraries.

2 To provide a basis for continuation of self-education.

3 To develop initiative and independence.

4 To learn how to find books on some special subject.

5 To prepare surveys from world wide periodicals of some subject on which no book is sufficiently up-to-date.

6 To secure access to information on some subject outside one's normal interests.

7 To be able to find data as a basis for planning.

8 To study alternative views.

9 To survey current affairs in daily, weekly, monthly or other periodical literature.

10 To develop ability to judge the comparative merits of books.

11 To acquire knowledge, skill in using it, and experience in where to find it, upon which power for leadership is based.

12 To enjoy some general acquaintance with books, their individuality, scope and location.

It is very interesting to observe that Hutton's list of objectives shows awareness of the importance of the time-factor in the retrieval of information—the need for training in writing a survey (5) and the need for awareness in study (9). Similarly, Hutton stresses the need to be able to obtain information outside one's normal area of study. This must be even more important in the 1970s due to the enormous increase in transdisciplinary research during recent years.

The goals for library use instruction at the University of Colorado Libraries were set out as follows, by Lubans in 1973. 'In detail, upon leaving the university the students would measurably understand major physical arrangements of libraries (the classification and cataloguing systems); major tools of reference such as indexes and abstracts in general and specifically those in his area of endeavour; (Also the love of reading with which the student arrived on campus should be no less upon his leaving it)'.

The goals and objectives for library use instruction for school and public libraries are also of relevance in the formulation of goals and objectives for university libraries, as library use is a continuous process throughout the educational and cultural system; this has been very clearly pointed out in the NATIS programme. Among the objectives mentioned for national and international action are:

2: Stimulation of user awareness

In order to increase user awareness, appropriate bodies, including universities and other educational institutions should include in their programmes systematic instruction in the use of the information in all the elements of NATIS. Use of libraries should therefore be a part of instruction offered from the primary school level onwards so that seeking information becomes a normal part of daily life. The content of these programmes should be expanded as the advance through the educational system progresses.

4: Assessment of users' needs

Surveys should, therefore, be promoted by the control body through questionnaires and other means to determine the needs of users of information. NATIS should be designed on the basis of these analyses in order *to offer the type and quality of service hoped for by users.*

Examples of general aims for library use instruction with particular reference to the school library are taken from Lubans' book *Educating the library user* (New York, Bowker, 1974).

Hawaii School Libraries 1964:

General objectives of library instruction:

a creating a love of books and reading

b integrating the library in the school program so that the work of the classroom is enriched and made increasingly vital

c equipping the student with an understanding of the use of books as tools

d aiding the student in building attributes of good citizenship through the use of the library

e developing responsibility and good work habits through library service contributed by students.

Oklahoma Curriculum Improvement Commission, Library Resources Division and State Library Service Committee, 1969:

Each student should be guaranteed a minimum exposure to basic library procedure. Those who learn to use research skills successfully will find that they can satisfy curiosity, do independent reading and enjoy books, recordings, and other materials without continued guidance of teachers and librarians. If this knowledge is acquired early in life, children will feel secure in their approach to school and public libraries and later to college and university libraries.

Scrivener, discussing the general aims for university library user education, describes the following as a very good summary of what any programme might aim to achieve:

The details will necessarily vary in different situations but teaching should establish and promote those traditional skills without which no student can make adequate use of his library. First, an understanding of library arrangements, physical, bibliographical and conceptual. Secondly a knowledge of sources and of which will be appropriate in any given situation. Thirdly, the ability to interpret his own need so as to frame a relevant question. Fourthly an awareness of search techniques including the ability to devise serviceable routines. Finally, the student needs skill in the art of evaluating his sources and presenting his material.

Hartz expresses some of the main aims for user orientation as follows:

Any library orientation program . . . should be concerned with developing a pattern of habits that lead to information sources that verify or extend his knowledge.

Examples of aims suggested for user education programmes in the UK are:

To ensure that the user can exploit library resources adequately and to his own satisfaction.

To establish a link between the subject taught and the library resources available.

To enable users to make maximum use of resources of the local and national library system.

To develop in the user a confidence in the use of the library and in the library staff.

To give students practical experience of using the literature.

To enable the student to be independent in his information seeking.

Aberdeen and Bradford Universities both consolidate the aims set for their overall programmes by formulating in consultation with the academic staff objectives for individual courses.

The main goals for a programme of user education at Chalmers University of Technology Library have been formulated in the following way. After completing the user education programme the student should have obtained:

1 The ability to apply the principles of scientific communication to problems of information retrieval.

2 The ability to use the various tools available in the university library (and other libraries) in order to obtain information useful in connection with studies and later work, as and when required.

3 A sense of enjoyment in information searching.

The first of these goals could be described as cognitive—*why* to use a particular information or tool in a specific situation. The second goal is mixed cognitive and affective—*how* to use the various resources available, and removal of the fear of not knowing how to use the tools. The third goal is affective. It was hoped that if this goal was realised an attitude would be formed about information retrieval in subsequent work situations—a basis for continuing education.

Having formulated the broad general goals for the programme of user education, it was possible to draw up a number of specific cognitive objectives within the framework. These are described below, in order to illustrate an attempt to break down general goals into a series of limited objectives. In this description a distinction will be made between library orientation and library instruction, as discussed in chapter one.

Library orientation is concerned with enabling the student to become aware of the existence of the university library and the services available there (*what* is available) and enabling the student to learn about the general use of the library: *when* the library is open; *where* specific items are to be found; and *how* to actually obtain/borrow the material required.

Library instruction is concerned with enabling the student to obtain information required for a specific purpose by making full use of the resources and materials available at the library. It is concerned with problems of information retrieval.

Short term objectives for orientation

After library orientation the student should:

1 Be aware of the existence of the university library, what it contains and when it is open.

2 Have the ability to locate handbooks, encyclopedias, bibliographic tools, periodicals (on open shelves), dictionaries, the reprocentre.

3 Be able to distinguish between the use of the author catalogue and the subject catalogue.

4 Have the ability to use a closed access library and be able to fill in a requisition form for the three most common types of loan (books, journals, and parts of a series).

Short term objectives for introductory course in information retrieval (for third/fourth year students)

Instruction in methods of information retrieval is often given in two stages—an introductory course for undergraduates and a more advanced course for postgraduates. The following is a list of short-term objectives for an introductory course.

After completing the course, the student should have the ability to:

1 Understand the concept of the time pattern for information flow from producer to receiver.

2 Be aware of the existence of different channels of communication from information producer to receiver.

3 Recognise the different types of information search: current awareness searches, retrospective searches, fact or data searches, browsing.

4 Locate, select and obtain information relevant to a specific subject topic of his/her own choice (such as the undergraduate research project) by:

a) carrying out the logical stages in a retrospective information retrieval search:

definition of search topic

expression of search topic in a number of search terms

limitation of search with respect to extent and time

b) using the various tools available for information retrieval:

project catalogues

patent indexes

report indexes

indexes to congress publications

indexes

abstracts

reviews

bibliographies

subject catalogues

5 Present the information obtained in the form of a written list of references.

Additional specific objectives for postgraduate courses in information retrieval

Additional objectives for the postgraduate course were that, after completing the course, students should have the ability to:

1 Follow the logical sequence, or flow, of a computer-based information search.

2 Construct a suitable search profile (with the aid of a documentalist) for covering his/her programme of research.

3 Compile a personal record system, which will be of value in compiling an accurate and consistent bibliography in connection with thesis writing.

As a parallel to these cognitive objectives, the affective objectives expressed in the general goals two and three could be formulated.

After the programme of library education students should:

1 Want to use, and *actually use* (ie realise the value of) their university and other libraries in connection with their studies and future work:

a) as a place in which to work
b) as a place from which to borrow literature
c) as a place from which to obtain information relevant to their needs.

2 Experience interest and enjoyment in the process of obtaining information.

These goals and objectives for the programme of user education at Chalmers University were, after formulation, discussed with student and staff representatives from the six schools of engineering. Both students and staff expressed satisfaction with the goals and objectives, which were then used as the basis for the development of a programme of user education (see chapter seven).

CHAPTER THREE

Teaching methods and media
for library user education

THIS CHAPTER will describe a number of teaching methods and media. These will be considered in relation to factors affecting the learning process. The use of the various methods and media in library user education will then be discussed.

Teaching methods may be roughly divided into those which are suitable for group instruction, those suitable for individual instruction, and those suitable for both (see figure five).

Choice of teaching methods and media depends on the learning/ teaching situation, the subject material, the students and the teachers. No single method could be suitable for all occasions.

Factors affecting the learning process

Education was described in the previous chapter as a process which changes the learners. This process can be affected by a wide variety of factors. However, as has been pointed out by Hills, there are four main factors that affect learning in practical situations: motivation, activity, understanding, feedback.

These factors can be considered in relation to the programme of library education:

Motivation Instruction should be given at a point of high motivation, as for example when the student wants to obtain information in connection with a particular project.

Activity Active work on a problem—learning by doing—is likely to be more effective than simply being told how to do a particular piece of work.

Understanding Library education will be more effective if the student understands what he is doing and why he is doing it—that is, if new facts can be related to existing knowledge.

Feedback Feedback, information on the progress being made should be available to the student.

In addition, factors affecting the neurophysiological sensory input can be considered. Teaching methods may, for example, use visual or auditory stimulation, or a combination of both. Methods which make

Teaching methods   Type of instruction

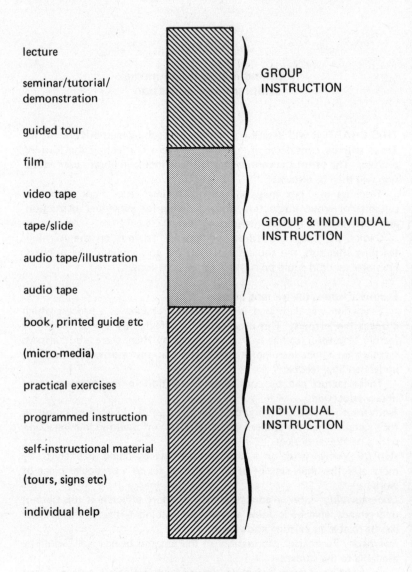

Figure 5: Teaching methods for group and
individual instruction
34

use of a combination of sensory inputs are likely to be more effective than those which rely on a single channel of communication. The possibility for the student to control the rate of flow of information, in a given learning situation, is another factor which affects the learning process.

Interaction between individuals concerned in the teaching/learning situation also affects the learning process. This interaction can be roughly divided into teacher-student and student-student interaction. Thus, for example as Revill has pointed out, in programmed instruction students work as isolated individuals; there is little or no interaction with other students, or with the teacher. This might be an advantage for some, but these factors 'may not favour the extrovert student who prefers the companionship and competition of the classroom. Research does indicate that introverts learn more easily from programmed learning than extroverts.'

In table two an attempt is made to consider various teaching methods for library education with respect to the factors affecting the learning process, the number of sensory inputs utilised, and student-teacher, student-student interaction.

From this it can be seen that no one method is suitable for all learning/teaching situations or for all individuals. The various methods and media should be used to supplement each other in any given programme of education. Enright has pointed out with regard to media that 'too much attention has been given to the possibilities of the new media supplanting the book, and far too little to the ways in which each can and does supplement the other'. The use of new media and methods may well stimulate increased use of other media and methods. Thus teaching by various means in a programme of library education may well lead to the increased use of media—both learning media such as books and tape/slide guides and media for information retrieval such as abstracts and indexes.

The timing of different aspects of user education

It is of great importance to provide instruction at a point when the student experiences motivation for learning about the material. The methods chosen for library user education should, therefore, involve the active participation of the student, at a point when he/she feels motivation to use the library, for example in connection with studies in some specific discipline. The student should be provided with information on the progress made during the problem-orientated activity.

Figures taken from an American survey indicated that 'learners retain about 10% of what they read, 20% of what they hear, 30% of what they see, 50% of what they see and hear, 70% of what they say as they talk

Teaching method	Factors affecting learning				Sensory input			Inter-action	
	M	A	U	F	Au	V	R	T-S	S-S
Lecture	±	±	±	−	+	+	−	+	−
Seminar/demonstration	±	±	±	+	+	+	+	+	±
Guided tour	∓	−	∓	−	+	+	−	+	−
Film/video, tape/slide for group instruction	±	−	±	−	+	+	−	−	−
Tape/slide for individual instruction	+	+	±	−	+	+	+	−	−
Book/printed media	+	+	±	−	−	+	+	−	−
Practical exercises	+	+	±	+	+	+	+	+	+
Programmed instruction	+	+	±	+	+	+	+	−	−
Self-instruction	+	+	−	+	−	+	+	−	−
Individual help	+	±	−	+	+	+	±	+	−

Key + = presence (of a factor etc)
  − = absence (of a factor etc)

M = the need for a student to be sufficiently motivated (Motivation)

A = the need for a student to be actively involved (Active work)

U = the need to relate new work to existing knowledge (Understanding)

F = the need for a student to evaluate continuously his progress (Feedback)

Au = auditory sensory input

V = visual sensory input

R = possibility for learner to control the rate of flow of information

T-S = teacher-student interaction

S-S = student-student interaction

Table 2: Learning methods—
a summary of factors affecting learning, sensory inputs,
and student-teacher interaction

and 90% of what they say as they do a thing'. On neurophysiological grounds one would expect there to be considerable differences between different individuals with regard to the most effective channels of learning; therefore, one must regard statements such as that quoted with a certain amount of scepticism. Nevertheless teaching methods which make use of a combination of sensory inputs are likely to be more effective than those which rely on a single channel of communication.

Traditional library instruction has made considerable use of the lecture method for large groups, the guided tour for smaller groups, and individual help to the student who asks for this at the information desk. During recent years there has been an increased use of audio-visual media such as tape/slides, films and video-tape, and to a certain extent computer-based instruction.

With regard to library education, table two shows that certain methods appear to be more suitable than others for this type of instruction. Such methods are small group methods—seminars and demonstrations, practical exercises, and programmed instruction. Other methods which should prove useful are lectures, the use of printed media, self-instruction methods, individual tape/slide instruction, and individual help. It appears that the guided tour and various audio-visual methods such as films and video-tapes would be less suitable. In the following sections the use of various methods and media for library user education will be considered in detail.

The lecture

Lectures are one of the traditional forms of teaching in higher education. They are used for teaching large groups of students and they make use of both auditory and visual sensory inputs (via the blackboard or overhead projector). The lecture method has the great disadvantage that the speed of delivery of information cannot be controlled by the receiver, and repetition is not possible unless printed handouts are provided, the student manages to write a synopsis, or some recording is made of the actual lecture. If attendance is voluntary, students who come to a lecture must feel some motivation. They play a fairly passive role, though the taking of notes involves the student actively in the learning process, particularly if an attempt is made to record the main points of the lecture in a logical sequence. The lecture gives the student a possibility to relate new facts to existing knowledge but provides no feedback as to whether this has occurred or not.

The lecture as a form of communication in higher education has been strongly criticised, not least by students themselves. Yet as has been shown by, amongst others, Hills, in an investigation of some applications of self-teaching systems, lectures do have considerable appeal for students. Attendance at lectures does not appear to be affected by the availability of outline notes. Both students and lecturers said that they felt that lectures gave an opportunity for personal contact. Students were able to note which points were stressed by the lecturer and staff were able to obtain some feedback from the students.

With regard to orientation in library use, Ford states that 'the lecture commonly given to freshmen students at the beginning of their first session, must surely be a waste of time. The library, with its vague connection with academic work, can hold little attraction for a student struggling to adjust to university life'.

What part could the lecture play in a course in information retrieval? The lecture must be a particularly unsuitable method for conveying information about bibliographic aids. Lectures about this type of library material tend to sound like a catalogue of unfamiliar names—the 'catalogue aria'. Accompanying illustrations are, even with the help of an overhead projector, difficult to make clear. However, lectures can be used as a stimulus, to present an overall view and to convey enthusiasm about the subject. Moreover, lectures can be used for groups of different sizes—an advantage in practical timetabling. Thus lectures might be suitable for providing a general introduction to a course on information retrieval.

Seminars, tutorials, and demonstrations

Seminars, tutorials, and demonstrations are given to smaller groups of students than the average lecture. The atmosphere tends to be less formal and there is greater opportunity for integration both between staff and students and between the students themselves. It is possible to provide motivation and to see that students are actively involved, say in a practical exercise during which they receive feed-back as to their progress. An attempt can be made to relate new information to existing knowledge. It is very difficult and extremely inefficient to explain the use of various specific tools for information retrieval in the absence of the source materials. This would be rather like trying to explain the use of the cathode ray tube in the absence of laboratory equipment or studying music without actually listening to it. Demonstrations might prove to be a good way of teaching small groups of about five or six students the use of various tools used for information retrieval. Students could be given the opportunity of actively searching for information about some topic in which they are interested.

The guided tour

The traditional approach to library orientation is the so-called guided tour, in which students are given a short tour of the library, during their first weeks as university students. Harlan has described a guided tour as follows: 'Batches of students—I have seen as many as thirty in a group are herded through a dozen or so stations. The guide is not

38

always a librarian, nor is he always well-prepared. "This", he says with a wave of his hand, "is the Periodicals Room, that", with a nod, "is CBI, a universal English language bibliography, dictionary arrangement with author, title and subject entries: You must remember that the main entry is author" . . . Small wonder that at the third and fourth station, most of the students stop listening. Libraries and librarians, they conclude, are as bad as anticipated. Obviously one's efforts are best applied in finding ways of avoiding, not utilising the library'.

The type of orientation described above, is often given when students have little or no motivation actually to use the library. The students themselves take little active part in the teaching/learning process, but tend to follow passively round the various stations. From the point of view of library administration the guided tour type of library orientation makes heavy demands on library staff time. There is also the problem, common to courses with high-recurrent frequency, of the guide remembering exactly what has been said to each particular group.

Audio-visual methods

During recent years there has been an increasing interest in the use of audio-visual media such as films, videotapes, tape/slide presentations, and audio tapes plus illustrated material, for the transfer of a moving sequence of events. In library education, however, there are few areas where it is necessary to use moving images. The information can be conveyed in a series of units such as slides or overhead transparencies or printed illustrations. This would suggest that the *tape/slide* medium or the use of audio tape in conjunction with printed material, as in the point-of-use teaching devices at the Barker Engineering Library at Massachusetts Institute of Technology, would be particularly suitable for library user education.

The advantages of tape/slide productions are:

1 Flexibility. Tape/slide productions can be used for both group teaching, as for example, an illustration of a lecture or seminar, or for individual tuition, as in preparation for a course or for repetition.

2 Constant availability. The use of the material does not depend on the presence of a lecturer or a librarian. It can be used by the student when the need arises.

3 The presentation of the material is not complicated. The tape/slide material is easy to project and easy to store.

4 Speed of presentation can be controlled—either by the lecturer in group instruction, or by the individual student.

5 They are easy to update.

It would appear that tape/slide productions, which enable colour to be shown, but not motion, are particularly suitable for use in library education programmes. They can be used in a variety of ways, combined with other methods of instruction such as lectures and programmed learning. They make use of a combination of two sensory inputs. Production costs are not too great and production can be undertaken at many libraries by the library staff themselves without external professional help. However, Hills found, in the investigation of self-teaching methods referred to above, that when tape/slide presentations were used as a substitute for normal lectures, these were 'not well received'. Both students and staff were critical of the impersonal nature of the tape/slide lectures. In contrast, when tape/slide presentations were used for individual instruction, students found them more acceptable. This favourable attitude to the individual use of tape/slide material has been observed in other studies. Individual presentation allows the student to control the rate of information and to repeat parts of the presentation, if this is necessary.

In Britain there has been a growing interest in the use of tape/slides, for library instruction, with the inception of the SCONUL cooperative scheme described in the next chapter. The use of a number of the SCONUL tape/slide presentations for user instruction has been experimentally tested on Swedish users. Swedish user reaction to the tape/slide medium were very positive and it was concluded that tape/slide presentations appear to be a suitable medium for conveying the type of information used in library education.

The use of other audio-visual media in library education should also be considered. *Filmstrips* possess many of the advantages of the tape/slide presentations, but they have a number of disadvantages, one being that the pre-set sequence compels the pictures to be shown in a given order. They are easily damaged—by scratching or heat—and are difficult to repair. They are also difficult to update. When one frame is outdated the whole filmstrip must be remade.

Films possess the ability to convey both motion and colour. However, in library instruction, one seldom has the need for conveying motion, and the use of moving images may well prove a distraction, rather than enhancing the learning effect. Everyone is familiar with the expensively produced ciné film, and library instruction films will be compared, usually to their disfavour, with commercial products. To make a successful film is time-consuming and expensive.

However, films can be used to create an atmosphere of reality, which could be useful for students prevented, say by distance, from visiting a certain university library. It is significant that the Open University in Britain made two films on the use of libraries—one showing the use of the public library and the other, produced for those students who were to attend summer school at some university, on the use of the university library under these conditions. The latter film has a playing time of twenty minutes. These films are technically well-produced and create an atmosphere of reality, useful for the student who has no opportunity actually to visit the library at the time of seeing the film. In the case of the Open University it is obviously worthwhile to produce well-designed audio-visual material that can be used for teaching thousands of students.

Video-tapes, like films, can be used to convey both motion and, in some cases, colour. They possess one considerable advantage over film material. It is possible to re-use the film, thereby making updating less expensive. However, it should be noted that updating of video-tapes is a time-consuming activity. Quality of product will, as in the case of films, be compared with commercial film and television products. Video-recording can be used, as with films, to create an atmosphere of reality and convey moving images, but these are requirements seldom met with in library instruction. Short video-recorded programmes might well be used to illustrate lectures, as a means for creating interest. Video-recording can make use of tape, film or discs for the actual storage of the recorded material. One of the problems facing libraries in the use of video material has been the lack of standardisation between different systems. It would appear that cassette systems are easier to use, as audio-cassettes, in library education. There are at present two types of TV-cassette systems, for play-back alone, and systems for both recording and play-back. The chief problem facing the purchaser of video equipment is the incompatibility between different systems. If standarisation were possible it would be easier to concentrate on the production of a series of high quality products for a wider distribution. Video recordings can be played on internal TV systems. The advantages of these methods are that they allow for careful preparation of material and can make use of the best teachers available. As the material is recorded it can be used many times. Internal TV systems can use displays suitable for audiences of different sizes. On the other hand the personal contact of the lecture, tutorial or seminar is lost. The student cannot stop the programme and ask questions and discussions may be difficult to organise; the instruction tends to place the student in a rather passive situation.

The book/printed guide

Printed information in book, compendia, or guide form has the advantage that it is available for use, as and when required. Individual students can work at their own speed, repetition is possible, and visual display in the form of diagrams is easy to achieve. What role can printed material serve in library education programmes?

Many libraries provide printed guides on the use of the library as part of their orientation programme. Such guides should always be written with the user in mind. It is essential to avoid the use of jargon.

If they are to be distributed to students the timing of this should be planned. Students receive an overwhelming mass of information during their first weeks at university, and this is not perhaps the best time to give out further material. Printed material can also be used for later stages of library instruction. These may take the form of 'Guides to the use of the literature in . . . ' The use of such guides for individual instruction meets the need for motivation—the student uses them when necessary. If the guides are consulted in order to find out how to obtain information the student has to work actively. A literature guide is based on some form of logical concept and should therefore provide the opportunity for the relation of new information to existing knowledge. If the guides are used in the active search for information a certain amount of feedback is provided, in that the student discovers whether he/she can obtain the information or not. Thus the provision of printed, subject-based guides to the literature could provide a useful method of library instruction.

Practical exercises

As can be seen from table two, students could be expected to learn well by actively carrying out a practical exercise, which they understand and in which they are interested. The importance of subject-orientated practical exercises in library instruction has been pointed out by, amongst others, Kolding Nielsen, who states that one principle for all forms of exercises must be that these should be, and be felt to be relevant to the subject. The seminars organised by the National Lending Library, on the use of literature in the natural sciences, medicine and the social sciences, also placed great emphasis on the use of practical exercises in library user instruction. It seems that practical subject-orientated exercises would be a very suitable method for library instruction as students feel motivation for active study and constantly receive feedback on their progress.

Programmed instruction

Programmed learning can be carried out by the user of a variety of media—books, automatic projection of slides, or by means of a computer-aided instruction (CAI). Programmed instruction possesses many advantages for library instruction. Students work at their own individual pace. They actively participate in the learning process and receive direct feedback as to the progress that they are making. It is also possible for the teaching staff to obtain a record of the student's progress. But students work as isolated individuals; there is little or no interaction with the rest of the group or with the lecturer. This might be an advantage for some, but as has been pointed out, the factor of isolation may not favour the extrovert student who prefers the companionship and competition of the classroom.

The use of CAI in library instruction has been developed largely in the USA. Axeen rewrote the material that she used in her course 'Teaching the use of the library to undergraduates' in fourteen units of instruction, each requiring two hours' use of the terminal. She compared the results of students who had taken the regular lecture course with those of students using the computer-based programme and found no statistical difference in the amount of learning. CAI library instruction has been used at a number of American libraries such as the Ohio State University and the University of Denver. As is pointed out by Clark, 'there is no doubt that writing long courses is time consuming' and the participation of the librarian 'should be confined to teaching library skills', leaving the programmer and educational technologist to work out the coding of the material. There is a great advantage in combining programmed instruction with practical exercises, as has been carried out by Wendt at Southern Illinois where use is made of a sample catalogue drawer. Computerised library courses certainly teach the student how to interact with the terminal and use computer dialogue. At MIT in Project Intrex use is made of the computer to teach the user how to carry out an information search. These early attempts point to a very interesting area for further development in library education methods. As greater use is made of the computer facilities for interactive information searching, it is particularly important to make use of terminal instruction programmes, which permit an optimisation of the interactive system at the man-machine interface.

Self-guiding material

Under this heading come such aids to library orientation and instruction as visual signs, colour coding and self-guided tours following a visual indication line. In the library it is necessary to make the user aware of the resources available and of their location. This can be achieved by the use of clear and attractive signs—a permanent visual display. Schemes of colour coding have been carried out in a number of libraries, notably Hatfield Polytechnic Library. Colour coding is used to reinforce clearly printed visual signs—thus material belonging to a certain broad subject area can be given one colour, subject matter pertaining to another subject area can receive a different colour and so on. Signs can also be used to indicate how to fill in a loan request form at a closed-access library, and for indicating how to get from one area to another. Self-guided tours can be used to provide library orientation. These often make use of coloured guiding lines. Commentary is provided either in the form of written instruction or in the form of an audio-visual commentary.

Individual instruction at the reference desk

The assumption is often made that the best form of library instruction can be given by the personalised service at the reference desk. This is because the student asks a question about the use of some part of the library when he/she is motivated to learn that particular point. The student is actively involved in the learning process and is receiving tuition from an expert. However, this idealised picture takes little account of reality. The reference librarian may be harrassed by several simultaneous enquiries, the telephone ringing, and so on. Many students are shy, and, if they see that the librarian is busy, don't like to explain that they didn't really understand what was being said. They hope that it will sort itself out with time—it is even more difficult to ask a second time. The real difficulty about this type of individual help is that it may provide immediate relief but not necessarily the understanding to cope with the same or similar situations in the future, though the case study in chapter six shows an attempt to remedy this situation.

During the evaluation of the undergraduate course in information retrieval at Chalmers Library, a series of interviews were carried out with students participating in the course as part of an attempt at illuminative evaluation. Among the unexpected aspects that came to light was this situation with regard to individual help. One of the students had tried to carry out a literature search during the summer, before coming on the course. He said that he had no idea how to use the catalogues:

S: I had to ask a librarian and I managed to use them, but it is an advantage to know how to use them yourself.

I: So you knew how to carry out a literature search before you came on this course?

S: Oh no, not at all, I had received help from the librarian before, but I didn't know any more for that . . . about the right techniques and so on.

The student went on to say that, though he had received help for a specific question, he had not obtained enough understanding to cope with his future library problems.

This interview was typical of the situation described by several students. The students, both in this series of interviews, and in another pre-structure evaluation interview, said that the main advantage of the course in information retrieval had been to give them an overall, systematic view of scientific information flow, which helped them to understand how to look for the information they required:

S: Well, the best thing about the course is, I think, that you get an all-round view of how it's arranged and the time aspect of the information flow—that it takes a long time for information to reach the books and compendia etc. You get an idea of the time perspective of the whole thing.

At most libraries student numbers have increased but there has been no corresponding increase in the number of librarians. As a result, there is rarely the time to provide adequate explanations as to why a particular step is carried out. In the words of Lubans, 'bibliographic first aid' only is provided. Thus it can be seen that individual help at the reference desk has both advantages and disadvantages as a method of library user instruction.

Summary

Choice of teaching methods and media depends on the learning-teaching situation, the subject material, the students, and the teachers. The methods and media for library user education should preferably involve the active participation of the student, at a point where he/she feels motivation to use the library. An opportunity must be provided for understanding—to relate new facts to exisiting knowledge. Students should be provided with information on their progress during their active problem-orientated work.

In practice a combination of teaching methods and media can be expected to provide the best basis for programmes of library user education, different methods being adapted to different parts of the programme and to the teachers and students concerned.

CHAPTER FOUR

Cooperative production of tape/slide programmes:
The SCONUL scheme

WITH THE development of user education programmes in the late 1960s came the awareness that considerable effort was going into the production of teaching aids, many of which duplicated each other. In particular, guides to the literature of a given subject field, to types of literature form (eg review serials), and to major sources (eg Beilstein), were almost entirely independent of the library producing the guide. One way to aid the progress of user education was, it was felt, to decrease this unnecessary duplication. A meeting was held in 1970 to discuss whether cooperation was desirable and what form it might take. It was thought that guides in an audio-visual format would add much to the effectiveness of the existing courses and could also serve as material for independent learning by individual students. The meeting concluded that the tape/slide medium was the most appropriate one for any cooperative scheme and a steering committee was formed to coordinate the effort.

The whole project was eventually brought under the auspices of the Standing Conference of National and University Libraries (SCONUL) as a working group, the aims of which were: a) to encourage cooperation in the provision of tape/slide guides to library services for higher education and academic research; b) to sponsor the production of such guides as effective teaching packages; c) to provide a forum of discussion among librarians, educational technologists and others engaged in this work; and d) to promote the dissemination of information on tape/slide guides through publication and other means.

Though there is some evidence to suggest that certain audio-visual methods may be better teaching media than others in the context of user education, the choice of method usually rests on administrative considerations such as ease of use, cost of production, etc, rather than instructional effectiveness. This explains the popularity and use of tape/slide as a method for library instruction. It is a cheap medium both in terms of production costs and of necessary equipment. Programmes are relatively easy to make and update. It is therefore a flexible medium compared with film and videotape for example. It can make use of colour far more cheaply than film or videotape but suffers from a lack of potential for movement. This is usually only a minor disadvantage in programmes for library instruction. Once produced the material is easy to use as the equipment for playback is reasonably well standardised and not, comparatively speaking, too expensive. This applies whether the material is used for individual instruction or for group viewing.

At the outset twenty-one university and two national libraries were involved in the development and production of thirteen programmes. An initial decision was made to base the development of programmes on the concept of a working party, consisting of representatives from two or three libraries either in geographical proximity or with special interest in the subject in question. The idea was that one member of the working party, and therefore one library, should be responsible for production of the programme but that during its development the other members of the working party should comment on the script and visual illustrations proposed and help assess the finished product. In this way any individual bias in one person's approach should be eliminated and the finished programme would be more likely to be acceptable to the wider audience involved in a cooperative scheme.

Standardisation is a prerequisite in any form of cooperative venture, not least one involving equipment, and it was necessary for the steering committee to issue recommended standards, for example for production of slides and tape recordings, or for mounting and copying of slides. Equipment was recommended for recording, editing, and pulsing of tapes and for replay of finished programmes. All these recommendations were laid down in a booklet produced by SCONUL in 1973 which also included guidance on the working party approach to cooperation, the preparation of teaching material and evaluation. The finished programme, when made available for sale, was to include a set of slides, a pulsed cassette, script, statement of target population and aims, and a copy of any notes or handouts for the student audience.

As with all user education the progress of the development of a programme depends to a large extent on the willingness and amount of time available on the part of the producer. In the early stages of the scheme the rate of progress towards completion of programmes was very uneven not only because of lack of time but also, in some cases, lack of production facilities. Nor were the stages involved in the production process always uniform from one production to another. It was decided that to give the finished products the degree of uniformity of approach and quality that might be expected from a cooperative scheme it would be necessary to use some form of evaluative procedure. The possible alternatives were seen to be some form of central vetting or the use of a locally applicable standard evaluation procedure which could be used during the development of the programme as well as on the final product.

47

The latter process was adopted and recommendations were made to producers. These involved production of a statement of target population, aims and objectives for the presentation and the production of questionnaires to measure the success with which the presentation was meeting its stated objectives in a learning situation with a suitable target population. Using this approach during the development of a programme allowed the producer to modify the programme as appropriate the better to achieve its objectives.

Diagnostic tests were also used in the formative evaluation process to indicate technical faults such as tone of voice, pace of presentation, academic level, quality of slides, etc. Much help on evaluation was given to producers at this time by a group working at the University of Surrey, who were in 1973 awarded a research grant by OSTI (now the British Library Research and Development Department) with the overall aim of investigating procedures and models for the preparation and evaluation of tape/slide guides to library instruction. It was hoped to refine evaluation procedures for tape/slide guides by evaluation of a number of guides by the project team collaborating with the producers. The project team acted as a catalyst to the promotion of exchange of experience between members of the SCONUL scheme. The wider aims of the project were to look at the integration of tape/slide material with other more conventional forms of instruction and to produce a reference index of aims and objectives covering the range of content of library instructional material.

As the research project at the University of Surrey commenced so a new round of productions in the SCONUL scheme were settled upon. This time thirty-five libraries were involved including some polytechnic libraries and the number of productions envisaged was seventeen. Progress was still slow though the number of completed programmes available for sale is now rising steadily with another new round of productions under way.

The choice of medium for the scheme was based largely on considerations of an organisational and administrative nature as explained above. In this context the scheme can be said to have been a successful cooperation venture. It has enabled many libraries and their users to benefit from teaching material that would otherwise not have been available in the local situation. In a wider sense though it might be seen that the scheme was too restrictive. In many cases with the medium already chosen, the message was designed to fit the medium. It would be more appropriate, in the wider context of user education, for the medium to be chosen in response to the requirements of the message. Fortunately tape/slide programmes produced in this way are not usually used in isolation but in conjunction with other forms of instruction and the drawbacks of adapting the content to the medium can be somewhat alleviated. The future development of a cooperative scheme will need to consider more closely the use of appropriate alternative methods depending on the task to be performed.

Some of the programmes available under the SCONUL cooperative scheme are listed below together with, in each case, the name of the library from which further information can be obtained.

Introduction to information retrieval in science and technology 41 slides, 20 minutes. Loughborough University of Technology.
Uses a small search as a case study to indicate and exemplify the basic steps of an information search.
Guide to searching British patent literature 52 slides, 18 minutes. Science Reference Library.
Discusses the identification of British patents and how to locate patents on a particular subject. Geared to facilities at the Science Reference Library.
Basic guide to the use of Beilstein 50 slides, 12 minutes. University of Salford.
Primarily intended for undergraduate and research students.
Guide to the use of Chemical abstracts 67 slides, 26 minutes. University of Southampton.
For undergraduate chemistry students with little or no prior knowledge. Intended to give a general awareness of what *CA* is and what it can do. Techniques of use of the various indexes are mentioned.
Guide to the use of literature in medicine and related subjects 80 slides, 17 minutes. Medical Library, University of Newcastle-upon-Tyne.
For those with no knowledge of the use of medical libraries. Covers the means of access to primary and secondary literature including computerised information retrieval.
Guide to British official publications 35 slides, 15 minutes. University of Warwick.
Particularly suited to courses in politics, public administration, law and librarianship. Introduces the nature and use of both parliamentary and non-parliamentary publications in a logical way.
Guide to the London Bibliography of the Social Sciences 35 slides, 20 minutes. University of York.
A guide to the use of the *Bibliography*, the subject catalogue of the British Library of Political and Economic Science.
Literature searching for management information 80 slides, 25 minutes. The Library, Management Centre, University of Bradford.
Case study illustrating the structure of the literature of management and how to search it. Primarily designed for postgraduates.

How to use Biological abstracts 41 slides, 20 minutes. University of Surrey.

Describes the function, content and arrangement of *BA* including the use of each of the various indexes.

Introduction to the literature of politics 80 slides, 25 minutes. University of Hull.

Aimed at first year research students. Describes the structure of the literature, illustrated by a simulated search.

Economic statistics: a case study 49 slides, 13 minutes. University of Lancaster.

By means of a case study enquiry based on the motor industry, some of the major types of statistical publications available in the UK are introduced.

Searching the literature of science education 58 slides, 30 minutes. Chelsea College, London.

Population census of Great Britain 45 slides, 30 minutes. University of York.

Covers the historical development of the census, the 1971 census, and identifying and using census papers in libraries. Illustrated with archival and published census documents as well as expository materials.

Introduction to information retrieval in the social sciences 2 parts: part I 62 slides, 20 minutes; part II 61 slides, 20 minutes. Loughborough University of Technology.

Suitable for second year undergraduates or new postgraduates, with the aim of improving library and communication skills.

Introduction to Science citation index 41 slides, 20 minutes. Institute for Scientific Information (Europe).

Explains how *SCI* is constructed and describes its main sections with detailed examples.

The literature of computers 55 frames, 12 minutes. City University, London.

Case study of a search for information on computerised traffic control.

The literature of economics 63 slides, 24 minutes. University of Essex.

Detergent pollution of water: a model literature search 49 slides, 18 minutes. University of Sheffield.

How to use reference books 2 parts: part I 40 slides, 8 minutes; part II 26 slides, 5 minutes. Polytechnic of North London.

Part I considers reference books relating to facts and figures; part II examines works relating to people and places.

Law reports tape/notes: part I 18 minutes; part II 14 minutes. University of Hull.

Part I covers the Incorporated Council of Law Reporting, *Law reports*, and part II reports issued before 1865, commercially produced reports and specialised series.

Other programmes which have been produced under the SCONUL scheme but which may not now be available except perhaps from the British Library Lending Division, include the following:

Introduction to the literature of sociology 28 slides, 16 minutes. University of Bath.

Outline guide to the literature of chemistry 50 slides, 16 minutes. Royal Holloway College, London.

Outlines a method of literature searching leading through the basic structure of chemical literature in a logical sequence.

Guide to abstracting and indexing services 32 slides, 12 minutes. University of Surrey.

Intended for students who have not used abstracts and indexes previously.

The literature of law: an introduction for students 80 slides, 25 minutes. Trent Polytechnic, Nottingham.

Intended for first year students of English law.

Finding out in geography 34 slides, 12 minutes. Polytechnic of North London.

Description of a literature search on forestry in Scotland for second or third year geography students.

Teaching packages for engineering students 6 packages including slides and ohp transparencies. Trent Polytechnic, Nottingham.

For use by third and fourth year students. Case studies on literature searching for electrical, production and design engineers and the literature of electrical, production and mechanical engineering are covered.

Programmes in the course of preparation include: *The literature of theses* (University of Manchester), *The use of periodicals and their indexes* (University of Exeter), *The literature of audio-visual materials* (Polytechnic of the South Bank, London), and *The literature of music* (Polytechnic of North London).

Guides on the following subjects are in the early stages of discussion as to format, etc: environmental sciences; compilation/citation of references; social statistics; art and design; American studies; literature of civil engineering; literature of electrical engineering; EEC documents; literature of education; company information.

Several tape/slide packages have been produced outside of the SCONUL scheme. Information as to their present availability is not known.

Index medicus 50 slides, 10 minutes; and *Using Hospital abstracts* 44 slides, 10 minutes. Enquiries should be addressed to: Area Library, Wessex Regional Library and Information Service, Southampton General Hospital, Shirley, Southampton.

Personal indexes 28 slides, 19 minutes. University of Sheffield.
Describes various methods by which collections of references can be organised and used.

Beyond the reading list: guidelines for research in the humanities University of Sussex.

The IUP reprint series of British parliamentary papers University of Sussex.

Introduction to the Social sciences citation index 47 slides, 25 minutes. Institute for Scientific Information (Europe).
Explains how *SSCI* is constructed and describes its main sections with detailed examples.

CHAPTER FIVE

Evaluation
in a user education programme

THIS CHAPTER provides an introduction to evaluation in library user education. The purpose of evaluation is discussed and is followed by a brief description of the targets, scope, methods, and timing. Examples of previous evaluation of library user instruction are then given. The final part of the chapter gives an account of the evaluation work carried out in connection with the development of a programme of user education at Chalmers University of Technology Library. This example of evaluation is related to the parameters laid down in the first part of the chapter.

Evaluation has been described in many different ways by educational research workers. Many of the definitions given are very general, for example that of Scriven—'evaluation attempts to answer certain types of questions about certain entities'. This type of definition is not very helpful for an understanding of evaluation. Evaluation is concerned with the collection of information about the effects of an educational course or programme. It often involves the comparison of observed effects with expectations or intentions. It is important to consider why evaluation is carried out, when attempting to understand what evaluation is.

Evaluation is concerned with the collection and analysis of information about the input, in terms of education potential, the variables affecting the educational process, and the end product or output. Evaluation can be directed towards the various aspects of the educational course or programme. Thus attention may be focused on the educational process of on the output or product of this process. The purpose of evaluation is to collect and analyse information that can be used for rational educational decision making. This definition of the role of evaluation does not include the element of judgement, which is part of educational decision making. Stake has pointed out that 'most evaluation specialists have chosen not to judge' even though many educationalists try to get them to do this. Scriven has charged evaluators with the responsibility for judging the merit of an educational practice. He makes the point that it is not sufficient to ask 'How well does the course achieve its goals?' one must consider whether the goals are worthwhile or not: 'How good is the course?' The latter question is concerned with a judgement of the aims of the course rather than with the functioning of the course. It is apparent that course evaluation and judgement of aims both form part of the wider area of educational decision making. Many recent evaluation studies do include a judgement element.

The purpose of evaluation has been described by Astin and Panos as follows: 'the fundamental purpose of evaluation is to produce information that can be used in educational decision making'. Educational decisions (like other administrative decisions) involve choices between available alternatives which are based on both educational and economic factors, and which often involve subjective judgement and value decisions. The role of evaluation is to provide information which can be used for rational decision making. Thus evaluation can be used for decisions about whether to continue or terminate a given course, about the modification necessary for an existing programme, about the use of various teaching methods to achieve a pre-specified goal, or about the adoption of an innovation.

The targets of evaluation

An education course or programme can be diagramatically represented as in figure six. Evaluation can be directed towards the educational process and/or the educational product.

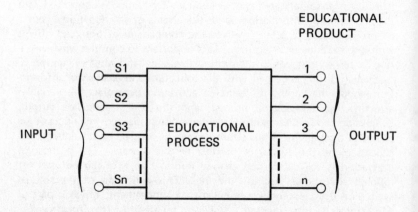

Figure 6: Relationship between educational process *and educational* product
S = student input (state of pre-knowledge) etc

54

The scope of evaluation

Evaluation may be carried out with regard to specific educational courses or to general educational systems. An example of the latter is Husén's *International study of achievement in mathematics*, where the aim was to evaluate differences in student achievement in mathematics in twelve different countries, with regard to such variables as school expenditure, teacher training, type of school organisation and degree of urbanisation.

A distinction may be made between assessment and evaluation. *Individual assessment* is concerned with the specific achievement of the individual student with regard either to his contemporary student group or to pre-specified goals. *Evaluation* is concerned with the effects of a given educational course, programme or system. In terms of figure six, assessment is concerned with individual output measurement. However, as can be seen, total individual output for a given course, with regard to pre-specified goals, can be used in the measurement of the effects of educational processes, if other variables are controlled.

Methods of evaluation

Evaluation can be classified according to the method used for the collection and analysis of information. Three main types of evaluation can be described (cf Howe and Delamont): the psychometric; the sociological or management; the illuminative or responsive.

Psychometric evaluation

Psychometric evaluation has evolved from the psychological discipline. During the latter part of the nineteenth century and the early part of the twentieth century, the application of quantitative methods of science was extended to psychology and so to education. This period saw the development of the 'test' phenomenon, which culminated in the test boom of the 1920 to 1930 period. Enthusiasts regarded the tests as providing 'objective' information which could be used in assessing the efficiency of a given educational programme or of the teachers. Psychometric evaluation is based on the assumption that it is possible to expose experimental and control groups to different treatments, while all other variables are controlled, and to measure changes by means of psychometric tests, achievement tests or attitude scales. Thus the experimental group may be exposed to a new type of physics course, whereas the control group follows the traditional course; in every other respect the two groups are exactly comparable. Pre-tests and post-tests are given to both groups, and the analysis is concerned with establishing significant differences in the performance of the two groups. These are then attributed to the variable being studied—the new course. This method assumes that 'irrelevant' variables can be controlled, an assumption

55

which is, in many cases, completely unjustifiable. In addition, this evaluation procedure is concerned with measuring output in terms of pre-specified goals and no attention is paid to unexpected effects.

Sociological evaluation

The management or sociological approach to educational evaluation has developed from the discipline of industrial sociology. This method is used in the study of changes in the structure of an organisation or the roles of the participants in an educational programme or a specific institution. This type of evaluation makes use of interviews and questionnaires. Participant observation is employed in many cases as a complementary method. Attention is focused on the organisation undergoing change, rather than on comparison with any control group. A recent example of the sociological approach to evaluation is to be seen in Gross's study of the fate of an educational innovation in a specific American primary school.

Illuminative or responsive evaluation

During recent years there has emerged a third type of evaluation which emphasises participant observation and interviews as a means to obtaining an overall view of education programmes. This type of evaluation has been called illuminative evaluation by Parlett and Hamilton, and responsive evaluation by Stake. Illuminative evaluation is not limited by the initial formulation of aims, but allows for the expression of unexpected results. The actual implementation of an innovation is regarded as the most important part of the study. Research is focused on what is actually happening in response to the innovation. Illuminative evaluation is concerned not so much with testing an educational programme but rather with describing and understanding the way in which the programme works, and how the participants are affected by it. Observational studies and explorative interviews are often used to obtain this information. Questionnaires and achievement scores may be used but they are rarely given high priority. One objection that is raised with regard to this type of evaluation is the difficulty of being objective.

The timing of evaluation

Scriven has pointed out the distinction between *formative* and *summative* evaluation. This distinction is partly based on the timing of the evaluation, and partly on the purpose for which it is intended: formative evaluation is carried out during the development of a course or programme and provides direct feedback about the functioning of the different parts of the programme, thereby giving information which can be used to modify the educational process. Summative evaluation is concerned with the evaluation of the educational programme as a final product. Thus formative evaluation provides information which can be used to improve a course, whereas summative evaluation can be used to provide information about the overall worth of a given course, to help in the decision as to whether or not the course should be continued.

Discussion

The learning/teaching situation is usually complex and dependent on a variety of factors, many of which are random and unpredictable. Evaluation of the functioning of an educational programme closely parallels the situation in medical diagnosis—evaluation of the functioning of a complex individual. In both cases it may be difficult to acquire sufficient information for a complete evaluation of the situation. The actual evaluation/consultation is a factor that may affect the existing situation. In both cases decisions may have to be taken as a result of the information collected. In educational evaluation one may attempt to avoid the judgement aspect—but decisions may then have to be made by some other group, decisions that will be influenced by the information collected and its presentation.

Certain parts of this information can be collected by means of tests, for example in medical diagnosis, blood-pressure measurements, heart-rate etc, but other information has to be collected by observation and by means of case-histories. All these ways of acquiring information are valuable and complementary—they contribute to an evaluation of the total situation. Each method has limitations; it is possible to collect detailed information by means of tests, but if the tests are concerned with some aspect that is of little relevance to the total situation, then the value of the results will be limited. In many cases it is extremely difficult to carry out tests under truly controlled conditions, because the external conditions are changing throughout the time-period in question. An example of this is to be seen in a developing educational programme. Detailed observations and discussion provide valuable information but they are time-consuming and therefore expensive. The evaluation methods chosen will depend on the purpose of the study and the resources available. However, the greater the variety of the methods used, the greater will be the chance of obtaining a complete picture of the educational course being evaluated, as the interaction of the various methods will produce a 'triangulation' effect—the same question being answered in different ways.

The need for the evaluation of library instruction

From the general account of evaluation given above, it will be obvious that all teachers evaluate. Attempts are made to improve existing courses, either as a result of personal observations, or from discussions with participating students. During recent years, librarians have become more aware of the need to evaluate programmes of library instruction. For example, Revill states that 'there is a great need for proper evaluation of the various teaching methods adopted in the library', and Lubans has pointed out, in 1972, that 'the results of evaluation not only present possible alternatives for better programmes but should also provide standards of performance for such instruction.' Yet the same author said, in 1974, that 'instructional programmes in all types of libraries have been infrequently evaluated, their need and effect have not been measured except in a few isolated cases'.

It would appear that, while many librarians are agreed on the need for, and the value of evaluation, with regard to user instruction, few have actually carried out systematic evaluation.

Previous evaluation of library user instruction

The learning/teaching situation implicit in library instruction is complicated and the goals and objectives envisaged by students, academic staff and librarians often differ. This is particularly marked in the formulation of the broad aims and goals for a programme of user education.

It is, therefore, perhaps not surprising to see that many of the evaluation studies described in the library literature give accounts of the evaluation of specific methods and media, which have been used in library instruction rather than evaluation of programmes of instruction. An example of such evaluation can be seen in the studies on the audio-visual 'point-of-use' aids developed at the Barker Engineering Library at MIT, and described by Stevens and Gardner. Similarly, an evaluation of tape/slide instructional programmes 'How to find a book' and 'How to find a periodical' has been carried out by Lubans at the University of Colorado Libraries. A research programme concerned with the evaluation of the SCONUL tape/slide instructional programmes produced by a number of British university libraries, has been carried out, from 1973 to 1975, at the Institute for Educational Technology, University of Surrey. In this evaluation project great emphasis was placed on the formulation of specific objectives. Use was made of pre- and post-instructional tests to measure short-term learning performance with regard to these objectives. User attitudes to specific presentations and to the tape/slide method of instruction were also studied.

The use of videosonic machines for library instruction was examined by Genung in 1967. The effects of computer-assisted-instruction in libraries has been studied and evaluated by, amongst others, Axeen, and Hansen. These evaluations have been directed towards the educational process in a specific learning/teaching situation and psychometric methods have been used to collect and analyse the information.

Psychometric methods have also been used in comparisons of two or more methods of library instruction, but in these cases the evaluation has been product-directed. Kirk compared two methods for instruction of students in introductory biology: lecture-demonstration and programme instruction. This evaluation was carried out by means of performance studies and examinations on library skills and the measurement of students' attitudes towards the programme. Kirk concluded that neither of the two methods showed superiority over the other. Kuo carried out a comparison of six versions of library instruction—lecture, audio-taped lecture, tape/slide presentation, television presentation, audio-visual instruction, (audiotutorial plus follow-up lecture, using overhead transparencies), and audiovisual instruction followed by a discussion with a librarian. Results indicated that the combination of self-paced audio-visual study, followed by verbal discussion with a librarian, was the most effective way of increasing student achievement in the ninety question test designed to measure course retention. It is interesting to observe that Kuo found that the slide presentation of visual material was more effective than television presentation of the same material.

Psychometric tests which attempt to measure students' ability to use the library have been developed and made use of primarily in the USA. These tests have been used for individual student assessment and as instruments for the product evaluation of instructional programmes. The most widely used of these tests have been described in a review by Bloomfield. One of the tests constructed during the 1930s is the Peabody Library Information Test designed by Shores and Moore. Another widely used test is the Feagley Library Orientation Test for College Freshmen designed in 1955 by Ethel M Feagley and others. Attempts have been made to compare various tests and to examine their reliability and validity. Thus the Peabody Test was examined by Deer, in 1941, using 1300 students. He concluded that the test gave satisfactory results for diagnostic purposes. Perkins carried out a study, in 1964, on the determination of the correlation between the Peabody and the Bennet Library Tests. Correlation was found to be as low as 0.385.

Criticisms of this type of library test can be made. They are artificial and do not adequately measure the students' ability to use the complex information tools available and thereby gain the information that would be of use for their studies. The question can be raised 'What do the library tests actually measure?' Bloomfield states that librarians have so constructed tests on library skills that it appears that 'we librarians have a poor understanding of the value of the library for our students'. Thus emphasis has often been placed on the use of the card catalogue as a major source for locating material, out of all proportion to its value for obtaining information when compared to other tools for information retrieval.

The difficulties in the design of suitable tests for library use—in the obtaining of information that is of interest to the user—may well be partly due to the aforementioned confusion of objectives between librarians, academic staff, and students.

However difficult it is to measure short-term effects of library instruction, it is far more difficult to measure the long-term effects of the instruction given. The long-term effect on the student and his/her ability to obtain information, is, however, of much greater interest than the measurement of short-term skills with regard to the use of specific bibliographic tools.

Evaluation studies at Chalmers University of Technology Library, Gothenburg, Sweden

During the last three years, a three-stage programme of user education has been developed at Chalmers University of Technology Library. This programme consists of: orientation for new users; an introductory course in information retrieval for undergraduates; and an advanced course in information retrieval for postgraduates.

The programme was evaluated in a number of different ways, in order to produce a triangulation effect and thereby obtain as full a picture as possible of the functioning of the courses. As the programme of library education was in a state of active development, many of the methods used were intended to provide formative evaluation on which course modifications could be based. The part of the programme which had received highest priority was the introductory course in information retrieval for the engineering undergraduates. As a result there was a corresponding concentration on the evaluation of this course. The following evaluations were carried out in connection with this programme.

Evaluation of tape/slide material for user instruction

A number of audio-visual tape/slide presentations dealing with various aspects of library user instruction had been produced under the SCONUL tape/slide programme, at a number of British university libraries.

These presentations are often subject-orientated and the text commentary is always in English. If it were possible to use this audio-visual material for Swedish students, direct with the English commentaries, it would save considerable time and expense. For this reason, it was planned to carry out evaluation of this type of material by comparing the performance of an experimental group using a Swedish audio commentary, with the performance of a control group using an English commentary. In all other respects the two groups were identical. Pre- and post-tests were administered to both groups and test performance was examined. Attitude questionnaires were also filled in by both experimental and control groups. This evaluation is an example of the use of psychometric methods, directed towards a given medium, or process.

The evaluation was carried out in order to provide information for a decision as to whether or not this type of material could be used for the user instruction programme at Chalmers University Library. It was concluded that it was fully justifiable to use English language tape/slide guides directly, without translation, for Swedish users. Users also stated that they liked this type of audio-visual material for library instruction.

Evaluation of the undergraduate course in information retrieval

The aim of the various evaluation procedures carried out was primarily to provide direct feedback on the innovatory user instruction course. Information collected and analysed could then be used to modify the course. Emphasis was on formative evaluation in connection with the educational process in a specific undergraduate course. Various methods of evaluation were used and these will be briefly described.

A Attitude measurement

Studies of student attitudes with regard to course content, instructional material, teaching methods, and the organisation of the course were carried out. Students were asked to complete, anonymously, after each course, a three page questionnaire dealing with the above-mentioned aspects. In this way students were enabled to compare their observations with their expectations. This evaluation was directed towards the educational process and made use of the psychometric approach. The evaluation was of the formative type.

B Evaluation by achievement

Performance measurement was carried out after each series of courses, by means of examination of each student's list of references, in order to see whether the students were able to carry out a practical literature search. Evaluation was directed towards the product of the course. Summation of the individual student assessments, according to groups with different motivation as, for example, work on an undergraduate research project, enabled the effect of motivation on performance to be studied. These student assessments were used as part of the formative evaluation of the course, in that they provided information on the functioning of the course as, for example, in the presentation of the references.

C Evaluation by pre-structured interviews

Pre-structured telephone interviews were given to a random sample of students who had taken part in the undergraduate course in information retrieval. These interviews were intended to provide information as to how well specific objectives, such as the awareness of the tools for information retrieval, had been achieved. In this evaluation study, psychometric methods were used to examine the product of the course in information retrieval. The interviews were carried out some ten months after the initiation of the courses, and included students who had taken part in some twenty courses. Some modifications were made to subsequent courses as a result of information collected—formative evaluation. The evaluation could also be regarded as being of the summative type, in that information was given of the functioning of a nearly finalised course.

D Illuminative evaluation

An attempt to carry out an illuminative evaluation of the undergraduate information retrieval course was also made. Detailed observations were carried out on the behaviour of the students during the actual course, and both students and teachers were interviewed as to their feelings in participating in this form of instruction. It was hoped that these detailed observations and interviews would give information as to how the course was functioning as a whole and how the different parts were functioning. This was non-preordinate evaluation, in which it was possible to find out unexpected information. This form of evaluation was regarded as being a useful complement to the other types. The information obtained could be used for the modification of the course under development—formative evaluation directed towards the educational process.

Evaluation of the programme of user instruction by the study of changing patterns of library use

In addition to the methods mentioned above, which were used specifically to evaluate the undergraduate information retrieval course, an attempt was made to carry out a long-term study on the use of the library with regard to reasons for use, materials used, success in carrying out literature searches, etc. It was intended to see if the total programme of instruction-orientation, introduction and advanced courses in information retrieval affected the pattern of use of the library over a period of five years. As priority was given to the undergraduate course in information retrieval during the first year and other conditions remained nearly constant, any changes in the pattern of the use of Chalmers Library during that time could be attributed to the effects of the course of instruction. Measurement was carried out by means of questionnaires. Patterns of use obtained after the introduction of the programme of user instruction were compared with the pattern of use obtained for a control group before the start of the innovation. In this way changing patterns of behaviour of the users of Chalmers University Library, in response to an educational programme, could be studied. This is an example of the sociological method of evaluation being used for summative evaluation of the products of an educational programme.

Evaluation of the self-instructional orientation programme

Attempts were also made to evaluate the effects of the self-instructional orientation material, by means of observations of how students performed a series of tasks. Observations on the way in which the tasks were performed, the time taken, and discussions with the students about their problems in orientation were carried out in order to provide information for eventual modification of the programme of orientation. A combination of psychometric methods and direct observation and discussion was used. The purpose of the evaluation was formative— for the modification of the process associated with the orientational material.

Summary

This chapter started with a discussion on evaluation and its purpose, together with a description of evaluation according to the four parameters of targets, scope, methods and timing. The advantage of using several methods of evaluation for a given educational programme was pointed out. A brief review of existing work in library user instruction evaluation was then given and related to the parameters previously described. The need for evaluation was realised by librarians, and obviously some evaluation was taking place, but few systematic attempts to evaluate programmes of user instruction by different methods had been made. Against this background, the evaluation carried out in connection with the development of the programme of user instruction at Chalmers University of Technology Library has been described and related to the parameters previously given. Evaluation has been carried out in several different ways, in an attempt to study the value of the innovatory programme, and long-term measurement of the effects of the educational programme has been started.

Preliminary observational studies of the self-instructional material provided for library orientation has shown that the material provided was of help to new users, but that it did not, alone, supply adequate orientation information. The formative evaluation of the introductory course in information retrieval for undergraduates has provided information on which course modifications could be based, and this has resulted in a model which appears to function well.

CHAPTER SIX

Case study: University of Sussex Library
The role of a Readers' Advisory Service

THE UNIVERSITY OF SUSSEX was one of the first of the so-called 'new universities' to be established in the UK, receiving its charter in 1961. In common with many of the other institutions established at this time it was to experiment with, and be innovative in, its approach to higher education. Consequently nine schools of studies were established (African and Asian studies, cultural and community studies, English and American studies, European studies, social sciences, biological sciences, engineering and applied sciences, mathematical and physical sciences, molecular sciences) which transcended traditional departmental divisions. Not only was the organisational structure different but the educational emphasis was very much on less formal methods. Seminars and tutorials together with guided learning were more favoured than traditional lectures particularly in the humanities and social sciences, and continuous assessment was of equal, if not greater, importance than traditional examinations. The present student population is of the order of 4200 of whom 3200 are undergraduates (the ratio arts:science is approximately 2:1 for undergraduate students), and the teaching faculty numbers some 650.

The library

The library in a new institution of this kind must mirror the objectives of the institution and contribute towards the achievement of them. In the formative years much effort was put into building a collection of material for use by both undergraduates and research workers. Consequent upon the widespread use of reading lists given to students to prepare themselves for seminars and essays it was decided to provide a collection of books in multiple copies for student use. Originally the main onus for the development of this collection and the main subject collections fell upon subject specialist librarians. Their emphasis was not only on collection building but on providing the full range of services normally associated with subject specialists including the provision of information services and library instruction. Indeed the emphasis throughout the short life of the library has been on the provision of service to readers and particularly to undergraduate students.

That the library should be involved in user education was without doubt. The purpose of the university library was defined in 1970 as follows: 'to contribute to (the achievement of) the University's objectives in teaching, learning and research by providing services to meet its current and future book and other information needs, and to maintain systems for improving the effectiveness of those services in responding to the changing requirements of the University.' Some of the functions of the library that followed from this purpose were a) to assist users in identifying their book and other information requirements, and b) to provide guidance and counselling in the use of libraries, assistance with readers' enquiries and instruction in effective methods of handling subject literature and other information sources.

It was about the time that this definition of the library's role was promulgated that two other developments occurred which had a bearing on the provision of library instruction. After the initial period of collection building and the necessity for subject specialists it was decided to move over to a system of functional organisation within the library, each assistant librarian now being responsible for the organisation of a section of work (eg acquisition, periodicals etc) whilst retaining a subject liaison role. One of the sections created in this organisational change of 1969/70 was the Readers' Advisory Service. Its initial full-time staff complement was two with additional help being made available from other sections of the library to cover desk rotas etc.

Also in 1970 the University of Sussex was one of six institutions in the UK to benefit from the appointment of an information officer on a three year OSTI (now BLRDD) sponsored project. The duties of the information officer were 'to be responsible for education and training of academic staff and postgraduate students in the use of information resources'. While not directly concerned with introductory courses for undergraduates on library use the information officer was to give such assistance as she could to other library staff running such courses. She was also to promote effective use of information services, both traditional and mechanised. It was envisaged that these objectives would be met through both formal courses of instruction or seminars (with which the librarian and his staff would be associated) and through advice and assistance with information problems brought to her by individuals.

Library instruction

The information officer's role at Sussex was thus to expand the programme of library instruction and establish an information service. In both areas it was necessary to work closely with the Readers' Advisory Service staff. Library instruction at Sussex had developed along lines very similar to those recommended by the Library Association in 1949. The initial introduction to the library was provided in the first week of term to organised groups of new students. The groups, up to seventy or eighty in number, came to the library and were shown a fifteen minute tape/slide programme in the library's seminar room. This, too, was of the traditional pattern, being a factual presentation of the library's services and on its use, illustrated with suitable internal and external views of the building, long shots and close-ups of the collections and the catalogue etc. This presentation was followed by a short talk by a member of the library staff re-emphasising the use of the catalogue with the aid of photographic enlargements of 'typical' catalogue cards. There then followed a tour of the building in groups of up to twenty. The library guide, a sixteen-page A5 booklet repeating the information already presented in tape/slide or lecture form, was distributed. A pregnant pause followed the request for questions and then the students were free to go. The whole process lasted for a little over half an hour. No evaluation or assessment was attempted but it became increasingly clear to those involved that the exercise left a lot to be desired.

All four elements were designed to impart information, in many cases the same information four times over. As an educational technique overkill may have something in its favour. There was however no doubt that solid factual presentations at this stage were a waste of effort. The treatment was too superficial, the groups were too large and the whole relied too heavily on the student's memory at a time when he was struggling to adjust to university life and was being given a considerable amount of factual information, most of which he considered more relevant and vital than information about the use of the library. The problem was what could replace this format, what was required to 'provide guidance and counselling in the use of libraries'.

User education

Experience of several annual introductory sessions had left the clear impression that students arriving at the level of higher education had had little or no guidance in the use of libraries previously. They were not aware of the full potential of a library as an information source and had usually little idea of the role the library could play in their education. In particular they had little idea of the potential of the human component within the library, namely its staff.

A radical reappraisal of the aims of the programme for introducing new students to the library was begun in 1974. It was decided that most of the factual content of the programme would be dispensed with and replaced by a presentation which concentrated on achieving affective aims relating to the changing, or creation, of attitudes about the library. The image of the library as a helpful and friendly organisation had to be conveyed. As was noted in chapter one the student has to be confident

66

that the library staff is competent and willing to help him and must be able to seek help with complete absence of self-consciousness or diffidence. The impact of the first contact with the library was therefore seen to be very important in creating an impression. The programme of orientation in the first few days could not be abandoned. Moreover members of the library staff argued that to abandon the traditional factual approach would be unfair to the student who would be denied basic information about the library and would create problems for the staff who would have to deal with repetitive trivial queries from new readers all day long.

The reappraisal of the orientation programme coincided with the introduction into the programme of the library of visits from local sixth-forms. If a new approach to orientation were to be devised then its value could be assessed by studying the reactions of the sixth-form students to it. If it met with approval then it could be introduced into the programme for new undergraduates. The aim of the sixth-form programme was to ease the transition from school to university for students in the local area, at least as far as libraries were concerned. Experience had shown that such a transition was not always easy to make in the pressure of the first week at university. Would an approach to students at sixth-form level prove worthwhile in terms of the modifications of attitudes (and perhaps also of the acquisition of factual knowledge)?

The programme devised was for upper sixth-form students. About a dozen local schools cooperated and groups of twenty to thirty students spent a single afternoon (about two hours) in the library. It was decided that what was required was a programme stressing two major themes: a) that the modern library is not to be thought of merely as a collection of books, but rather as an active communication complex, demanding— but also rewarding—the expenditure of time and effort in mastering techniques of access; and b) that as a human component in this system the librarian himself provides an indispensable access point. The initial attempt to meet this aim was conventional. The Open University film *Using libraries: the university library* was followed by a twenty-minute talk aimed at relating the film's contents to the needs and expectations of the group. A conducted tour of sections of the library (audio-visual materials, periodicals, undergraduate collection etc) was rounded off by a period of question and answer. It was obvious from the reaction that this package was not accomplishing the ends to which it was addressed. It was necessary to return to the basic principle that in the learning environment discovery must take precedence over the ingestion of pre-packaged facts.

The basis of the present sixth-form programme is a series of fifteen assignments framed in such a way that the student answering any two or three of them will be introduced to a fairly comprehensive range of library resources, eg:

The work of the Kensington War Hospital Supply Depot is referred to in *Punch* for 13 November 1918. Using the name of the matinée organiser mentioned in this short note, find out, with the help of the *Times index* and back issues of the *Times* on microfilm, what in particular the hospital was noted for.

Compare the treatment of Cape Canaveral (Florida) in the *Faber atlas* and the *Times atlas of the world* (Comprehensive ed). Use *Encyclopaedia Britannica* to account for the differences.

The Tacoma Narrows Bridge collapsed in November 1940. First view the four-minute film of this incident which is stored in the Audio-visual Materials Room; then use *Encyclopaedia Britannica* to find out what caused the collapse and to trace one standard book on suspension bridge theory. Is this book in the library?

Students tackle assignments in pairs after a short introductory talk explaining the purpose of the visit and the showing of a tape/slide in cartoon format, on using the university library. Time is set aside at the end of each visit for discussion of questions like—what kinds of materials can be borrowed from university libraries? What is a typical period of loan? Do all university libraries collect tapes/slides/videocassettes? How do the opening hours compare with those of public libraries? etc. The enthusiasm which the majority show and their willingness to tackle relatively complex procedures, for example, using flow charts to explore the subject catalogue or following printed instructions for threading microfilm was surprising and caused some essential rethinking of the orientation programme.

Points emerging from these sessions, of value in preparing for new undergraduate students, were: a) the cartoon tape/slide with a dry-humour commentary was valuable in creating an atmosphere in which further instruction was accepted; b) it was not necessary to provide a lot of factual information about the library for students to begin to use it; and c) practical work, objectively set, was a valuable component in any learning situation.

With this in mind the orientation session for new students during their first week at the university was designed to incorporate the tape/slide presentation, suitably introduced, to create an atmosphere and the feeling that the library staff were helpful, friendly, but above all human. The tape/slide was supported by a tour of only part of the building where the major services were located and particularly the Readers' Advisory Service. Emphasis, though not unduly so, was put on the need to follow up the initial introduction with questions about the use of the library as they arose. The idea was conveyed that the service was a service of first resort for any questions concerned with the use of the library or library materials. A library guide very much reduced in size from previous years and containing only essential information, was distributed. However, it was felt, though not tested, that the motivation of the students would not be sufficiently high for them to use a similar sort of practical approach to that employed with the sixth-formers. In addition there was a problem of numbers and timing. Whilst staff could be made available to help two dozen students for an afternoon it was not possible to provide staff to deal meaningfully with one thousand students in the space of a week, given that one of the major objectives of this orientation session was to introduce a 'friendly' and helpful staff. Where, however, follow up sessions were arranged for first year students later in the first or second terms a similar approach was adopted.

To assist users to find their own way in the building, which has certain geographical complexities, and to provide information about the services provided by various sections of the library it was decided also to redesign the guiding and signposting used within the library. Up until this time the provision of guiding had concentrated mainly on labelling of the stacks themselves and insufficient attention had been paid to guiding the readers to those stacks. This had meant that at least 10% of the queries received by the Readers' Advisory Service had been for locational information. The redesigned guiding had to be flexible, to accommodate changes of library layout, and hierarchical. As near the entrance and the main traffic flow as possible was placed a plan whose main function was to give an overall concept of the building. A large perspective drawing approach was adopted for this purpose, using different coloured transparent overlays to represent different functional uses of areas of the building. Above the plan a key was provided giving a brief definition of the function of each of the service points shown on the plan so that the reader could ascertain which service point could supply his particular need. By the side of the plan was the main signboard showing the contents of each floor of the library including subject and classmark because the reader, progressing from the catalogue to find a particular book, is more likely to need the classmark approach. From this main signboard, which also served as a directory, the reader was guided by means of small arrows in the direction in which to proceed. As he turned in that direction he would see the next signboard and so on until he reached the necessary area of the library where he would find detailed local plans of that area to enable him to locate on the shelves the material he required.

Guiding was seen to be an integral part of the provision for the orientation process. However the orientation programme outlined above, for students in their first few days at university, was very much setting the scene for the future. Its purpose was to give the students confidence in the library staff as being able and willing to help them on a continuing basis with their problems in using the library. The half-hour programme of the first few days was not seen as a one-off occasion for orientation but the beginning of an ongoing interaction between librarian and student on a one-to-one basis, with the student feeling able to seek help at a time of need. As this relationship develops the amount of help in use of the library will decrease and, as the student develops in his subject discipline, will be replaced by information of a bibliographical nature connected with the subject. The two forms of help cannot be separated, each encounter of librarian and student will have an element of orientation and bibliographical instruction. The important thing though is to deal with the student's own problem at the point and time of need and not to wait until an organised course can be arranged for a group. The process is a continuous one, not intermittent, as is the traditional pattern.

Despite the attempt to create the atmosphere for interaction during the initial orientation session not everyone who needs help will ask for it. For this reason the traditional formal courses of instruction have not been abandoned. They are used at appropriate times, usually prior to the student's project or long essay in the second or third years, to supplement the personal and individual informal education. In this provision the library reacts to expressed demands and provides courses covering the literature and access to it for given subject fields. Much emphasis, though, is again placed on the help available when individual students encounter problems with their own literature work.

The help provided for individual students is not typical of reference desks in many libraries. The aim of the Readers' Advisory Service is not to dispense pre-packaged items of information on demand, rather it can be seen as presenting the student with the raw materials and an instruction manual enabling him to assemble the parts, not only of that design model, but of similar ones he may need later. In other words work is not done for the student, rather it is done with him using his expressed problem as an instructional medium to transmit points of principle relating to the use of the library or the literature. This approach operates at all levels of enquiry, from the obvious and frequently recurring problem of catalogue use to the compilation of bibliographies. For this reason the Readers' Advisory Service does not undertake literature searches as such for students. Whilst suggesting sources likely to produce relevant references, assisting in their use and advising as to possible subject headings, etc, the service will not actually compile the bibliographies. In the words of the Chinese proverb, give a man a fish and he will have a meal, teach him how to fish and he will eat all his life.

The main requirement for the effective operation of an informal advisory service of this type is manpower, not in terms of number alone

70

but in terms of personality and ability to communicate easily and naturally with students. The service is however, manpower intensive, typically involving four people almost full time, two half-time and one other helping for one afternoon per week. Since very many of the queries received are of a subject nature, as well as orientational, it is necessary for this staff complement to have varying subject backgrounds. The service operates from a desk in the central area of the entrance floor of the library. It is located immediately adjacent to the catalogues and close to the main guiding display described above. It is clearly visible from the main traffic route into the library. A rota operates for the manning of the desk but since any query is likely to involve moving away from the immediate area it is necessary to have other members of the service available to step in and provide continuity of service.

The time taken on an individual query depends very much on its nature and can take anything from a few seconds up to half an hour or so. If the query relates to location of information on a topic and it is likely to take considerably longer than this to locate relevant sources then an enquiry sheet would be filled in. This would be dealt with by members of the service not manning the desk and the reader contacted and invited to call in for further assistance. At other times members of the service, when not at the desk, would be preparing support material in the form of booklets designed to be supplementary to the individual help given. These are freely available at the desk also. The number of queries received per day by the service varies from about one to two hundred, depending on the time of year. The type of query received is typical of any library ranging from 'how do I look up Müller in the catalogue?', which might take only a minute or two to demonstrate and explain, to 'what material has been written in the last ten years on the effect of altering marine propellor pitch and its control?', which might take an hour initially followed by further periods as the student's searching progressed.

The function of the library in providing guidance and counselling in the use of libraries and assistance with readers' enquiries as well as instruction in effective methods of handling subject literature is thus being met in a variety of forms, though guidance and counselling on an individual basis is of prime importance in relating to the needs of the students.

CHAPTER SEVEN

Chalmers University of Technology
A systematic programme of user education

DURING THE YEARS 1973 to 1977, a systematic programme of user education has been developed at Chalmers University of Technology Library, Gothenburg. The background situation at the university will be briefly given, followed by descriptions of the four parts of the programme: library orientation; an introductory course in information retrieval; an advanced course in information retrieval; and seminars for industrial engineers.

Background

Chalmers University of Technology has approximately four thousand undergraduates and some six hundred postgraduates, who study in one of the six schools of engineering: school of engineering physics, school of mechanical engineering, school of electrical engineering, school of civil engineering, school of chemical engineering, school of architecture.

The undergraduate programme takes four to five years of study, with about fifty effective working hours per week, and leads to the first degree of 'Civilingenjör' (equivalent to MSc or MEng) or 'Arkitekt'. 'Studies in the engineering departments are usually organised in intensive, discipline-orientated courses supported by laboratory work . . . Heavy emphasis lies on training in problem solving'. (Olving, 1977) Further details of courses within the different schools of engineering can be obtained from the 1976 edition of *Some facts about Chalmers University of Technology* published by the university authorities. Graduate students work for a four year degree—Doctor of Technology. They are usually employed as assistant at the university, with full-time salary. About one year is spent on formal graduate courses and the remaining three years on research for a thesis.

Chalmers University is served by a main library plus a number of smaller section and departmental libraries. The main library has a collection of some 270,000 volumes. The number of currently held periodicals is 5300. Most of the collection is placed in a closed book magazine or 'book-tower' to which users do not have direct access. Material to be borrowed must be ordered on special order forms which contain information on the unit to be borrowed and on the borrower. The material requested, if available, is then taken out of the store and brought to the borrowing desk. This takes an average of about five minutes. At present, one of the main aims of the library staff is to convert the existing closed-access system to open access, thereby increasing the availability of the resources.

In 1971, students from the School of Engineering Physics asked the library staff to arrange for a course in library instruction. In response to this request an initial course of forty-nine hours was provided, which included library administration, principles of cataloguing and indexing, manual literature searching and report writing. This course attracted only a small number of students—about fifteen per year, and only two-thirds of these completed the course. In view of this it was decided to try to design and develop a course that was directly related to the needs of engineering students in their general course of studies.

User studies showed that very few (6%) of the undergraduates used the library as a place for optional studies, and that the majority (92%) considered that they bought most of the literature required for their studies. As so few of the undergraduates made use of the library for traditional purposes of study or for borrowing material in connection with their studies, it was asked how much they knew of the information resources available at their university library. It was shown that while 71% of the undergraduates were aware that the library possessed a subject catalogue, only 25% were aware of the existence of abstracts, 32% of the existence of indexes and 36% of interlibrary loan services. Of the undergraduates who knew of the existence of the subject catalogue, about half said that they either did not use it or that they experienced difficulties in its use. Students could hardly be said to make active use of the library, or to be aware of the information resources available there. Yet students commented, when being interviewed that they were interested in finding out more about the library and how to use it in connection with definite projects such as seminars or their undergraduate research project.

Against this background it was decided, in 1973, to develop a systematic programme of library user education. This programme consists of four parts:

1 Orientation for approximately nine hundred new users per year.

2 Introductory courses in information retrieval for third and fourth year engineering undergraduates (for about eight hundred students per year).

3 Advanced courses in information retrieval for postgraduates (four courses per year).

4 Seminars on methods of information retrieval for industrial engineers.

Aims and specific objectives were formulated for each part of the course (see chapter two) and suitable methods were chosen to implement the teaching at the various levels. A description of the practical organisation of the different parts of the course will now be given.

Library orientation

Library orientation, which is provided for some nine hundred new users per year, is concerned with enabling the user to become aware of the existence of the university library. As can be seen by a study of teaching methods (see chapter three), the traditional methods used for library orientation, the guided tour and lectures, do not seem to be particularly suitable for transmitting this type of information. It was, therefore, decided to make use mainly of self-instructional methods for this part of the programme.

Printed handouts

The first piece of information was sent out in the form of a single sheet, handwritten and reproduced by offset printing. This paper contained information likely to be of interest to the new student. 'At Chalmers University there is a library, where you can read *Yachting news* (and 4000 other periodicals)'. It contained information that there were study places for student use, and a reference collection of dictionaries, encyclopedias, handbooks and tables available for consultation, and that there was a reserve book collection of set course literature. It also contained information of the hours of opening of the library, and the vital information that there was a pleasant cafeteria.

The second printed handout was intended for students during their first term, and took the form of a sixteen page A5 *Guide to the use of Chalmers Library*. This guide described the services and resources available, the hours of opening, the location of the material, and how to obtain the literature required. The guide was written with the user in mind. Technical jargon was avoided throughout. It was produced in a size that would fit into a pocket or handbag, and there were a number of illustrations by two architectural students (see figure seven).

Self-guiding colour-shape coding system

A self-guiding colour-shape coding system was designed for the location of material available on direct access in the library. Schemes of colour-coding/shape-coding have been developed at a number of libraries, notably at Hatfield Polytechnic, Hertfordshire, England. The colour scheme at Chalmers utilises the different colours used by the six schools of engineering. With this scheme, material pertaining to the School of Electrical Engineering is coded with yellow symbols—the colour used by that school. Differently shaped symbols have also been chosen to represent types of material to be found in the library (see figure eight).

Figure 7: Line drawings from the 'Guide to the use of Chalmers Library'

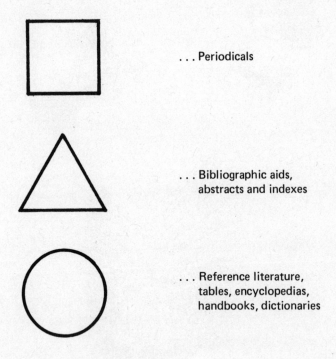

... Periodicals

... Bibliographic aids,
abstracts and indexes

... Reference literature,
tables, encyclopedias,
handbooks, dictionaries

*Figure 8: Symbols representing the different types of material
to be found in the library*

In addition to the location signs, other signs were made and put up, for example a sign showing how to complete a loan-request form,for the three most common types of material to be borrowed—books, periodicals, and continuations. This sign was hung above the author catalogues.

Tape/slide guide

A tape/slide guide to the use of the library was made. This presentation lasts for five minutes and describes the library and the material it contains. It explains that as the main part of this material is kept in a closed-access book store, it is necessary to fill in a loan requisition form on which the store location number is marked, in order to obtain material. The tape/slide guide was designed to meet both cognitive goals for library orientation and affective goals—realisation that the library could be a pleasant place in which to work and removal of the fear caused by a new strange environment and new borrowing procedures. This tape/slide guide has been used as part of a very short general introduction for freshers and as introductory material for various groups visiting the library.

Discussion

Preliminary observational studies on the use of the self-guiding material provided for library orientation have been carried out and from these it was concluded that the orientation material so far provided for students has been of help in the actual use of the library. However, this material alone, did not supply adequate motivation to encourage new students to come to the library. It did not provide new users with an adequate explanation as to why they should use certain catalogues or other resources. It has been seen that students at Chalmers made little use of the library's reading-room facilities, nor did they borrow material in connection with their university studies.

Motivation to visit the library can be provided in a number of ways—by arousing curiosity and interest, for example, by providing handouts and library guides, or by introductory lectures, or by stressing the availability of other services, such as the cafe. Motivation provided in this way may result in the students gradually becoming aware of the resources available at the library, but may not necessarily result in motivation to use the place.

During the first year at Chalmers many of the students, particularly those in the large schools (those of electrical and mechanical engineering) work in traditional large group lecture environments, with compulsory laboratory work. A considerable amount of time is spent on theoretical introductory studies such as mathematics. Against this background students suggested that first-year students could work in small groups on practical projects, where they would have to look up a certain amount of information. This would enable students to get to know a number of their fellow students, provide study motivation in the form of a practical engineering problem and provide the students with motivation to use the library to look up information. Since 1975/76 students at the School of Architecture at Chalmers have taken part in project-based courses, from their first year at the university. This has resulted in a considerable increase in the use of the architecture section library.

Plans have now been made for the introduction of small-group project-based studies for the two hundred students in the School of Mechanical Engineering, from the academic year 1977/78. Library orientation and use will form part of this project work. Discussions have also been held in the School of Electrical Engineering, as to the possibility of starting project work at the beginning of university studies. It is hoped that in the future library orientation can be provided as an integrated part of the normal course of studies at the university.

Introductory course in information retrieval

A basic plan was drawn up for a fourteen-hour introductory course in information retrieval for third and fourth year engineering undergraduates. It can be seen from chapter three that certain methods appear to be particularly suitable for library instruction. Such methods are small group methods—such as seminars, demonstrations, and practical exercises. Other methods which ought to prove useful are lectures, the use of printed media, self-instruction methods, individual tape/slide instruction, individual help, and programmed instruction. Methods to be used for the introductory course were, therefore, selected from those outlined above.

The course comprises the following elements:

1 A brief description of the rapid increase in scientific and technical publications.

2 Scientific communication—the different channels.

3 The forms for printed communication—with division into primary and secondary information sources.

4 Different types of literature search: current awareness, retrospective searches, factual searches, browsing.

5 Methods of information retrieval.

6 Use of different tools for different information retrieval purposes.

7 A practical information search centred on the student's own particular topic of interest.

Figure 9 is a plan of the course which consists of:

1 x 1 hour lecture—Introduction to scientific communication

1 x 1 hour lecture—Methods of information searching

2 x 5 hour 'laboratory' sessions at approximately a week's interval:

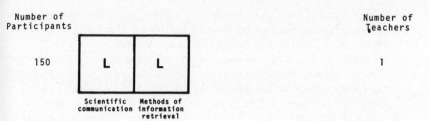

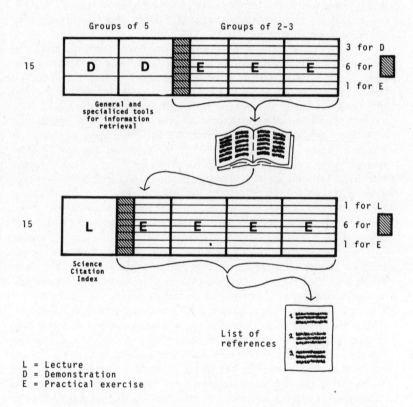

L = Lecture
D = Demonstration
E = Practical exercise

*Figure 9: Diagram of the introductory course in information retrieval
at Chalmers University of Technology Library*

a) conventional tools for information retrieval, such as *Engineering index, British technology index, Artikkel indeks*, plus subject-related tools. b) the use of *Science citation index* and similar tools such as the *Index to scientific reviews*. Starting point for laboratory session (b) is the reference list obtained during session (a).

2 hours 'home study' for the presentation of the list of references.

Lectures were used to provide an overall introduction, and to act as a general stimulus. The size of the group attending the lectures was about 100 to 150 students. Printed material was provided in order to help the students to cope with the rather rapid flow of information, much of which was given in the form of diagrams, which would have been difficult to notate. Use was made of a set of slides to describe the process of a literature search.

The laboratory sessions were limited to fifteen students, from the same school. During the 'lab' sessions, use was made of variable group size. Each session started with demonstrations lasting for about an hour. The students worked in groups of not more than five and, at the first session, studied the general layout of the library, the use of catalogues, etc, the use of general tools for information retrieval and the use of subject-specific tools, such as *Electrical* and *Electronics abstracts*. A common search theme was taken up, for example, the use of solar energy for heating buildings, the reduction of noise in machine-tool workshops, various aspects of water pollution etc. Students were provided with a handbook, *Guide to the literature in . . .* (their particular discipline). This gave illustrated examples of the use of the various tools, and was intended to serve as a future source of reference, as the need for information retrieval arose in connection with various work projects.

The most efficient way of learning how to carry out a literature search is almost certainly by carrying out an actual search on a topic in which one is interested—learning by doing. The main part of each 'lab' session was, therefore, devoted to a practical search carried out by the students, working in small groups (up to three or four) or as individuals. The majority of students searched for information useful in connection with their undergraduate research project (all students spend approximately three months working on a research project). At the start of the practical search, as many as five or six of the library staff were available to give help and advice—thus group size was about three students to every teacher. The purpose of this was that no student should have to wait too long before actually obtaining some positive result from his/her search. After the initial period of about twenty minutes, when all the groups faced starting problems, it was possible to use only one member of staff for the laboratory instruction. Problems during the latter part of the lab arose at irregular intervals and were fewer in frequency than at the start of the session. This allowed an economical staff/student ratio to be achieved. Students presented the results of their search in the form of a list of references.

Observations of the students at work during the laboratory sessions showed the importance of carrying out a search in which one is interested. It took students without a definite search topic four times as long as those searching in connection with project work to obtain their first reference.

In the second session use was made of the references obtained during the first session, to continue the information search with the help of *Science citation index.*

Evaluation

The introductory course in information retrieval was evaluated in a number of different ways—by means of studies of student attitudes, performance results, prestructured interviews designed to provide information with regard to achievement of the specific course objectives, and by means of explorative interviews with participating students and teachers. This evaluation work showed the course to be functioning reasonably well. Students themselves, somewhat to their surprise, appeared to enjoy their studies in information retrieval. As one student expressed this, 'Yes, of course it's a question of where one is working, but one thing is certain, I shall use the available libraries in a different way. I intend to try and go on from here . . . learn to find out more . . . and practise for myself.'

Comments have also come from industry. 'The engineers who now come from Chalmers know how to start to tackle a problem. They don't have to be told how to look for information. They go to work directly.'

Advanced courses in information retrieval

Thirty-five hour courses on information retrieval are provided for postgraduate research students. Teaching takes place for homogeneous student groups (that is from the same school of engineering) of up to ten students at a time. In this advanced course of information retrieval, emphasis is placed on the use of computer-based methods. The development of national and international data bases is described, together with the possibilities and methods for carrying out retrospective searches to obtain a comprehensive coverage of all the information available on a given subject, and for current awareness searches for updating with newly published information within a specific field.

The course takes place in concentrated form lasting about one week. The main part of the instruction is devoted to practical work:

1 Each user compiles a search profile to cover the subject of his/her research project. This profile is then tested experimentally for three months, with batch processing, on the EPOS-VIRA Selective Dissemination of Information Search System developed at the Royal Institute of Technology Library, Stockholm.

2 Each user carries out interactive literature searches on one or more of the following systems: LOCKHEED-DIALOG, ESA RECON or SDC-ORBIT—three information systems containing many data bases in science, technology, engineering, social sciences, economics and business. These systems can be accessed interactively for either retrospective or current awareness searches.

Part of the course is devoted to the written and spoken presentation of results. A seminar with discussion is devoted to various aspects of technical writing and the presentation of references.

The postgraduate students are highly motivated, and evaluation has shown that their attitudes towards the course are very positive.

Seminar for industrial engineers

In response to requests from individual engineers and organisations, one to two day seminars have been provided for industrial engineers on both manual and computer-based methods of information retrieval. The material and teaching methods used are selected and adapted from the two regular courses on information retrieval in accordance with the needs and wishes of the various groups concerned. Emphasis is placed on problem-solving searches carried out within the user's own expressed fields of interest.

Two of the schools at Chalmers University—Electrical and Mechanical Engineering—provide regular postgraduate programmes designed to update previous studies for practising engineers of some years' experience. It is planned to include a short course on 'New methods of information retrieval' in these programmes from 1978 onwards.

Chalmers University Library has been asked to provide library user education, on a contract basis, for the Swedish Atomic Energy Company, from the autumn of 1977. Specially designed courses will be given for different user categories, in accordance with the objectives specified by the representatives of the firm. Several other firms and organisations have also asked Chalmers Library to design and provide courses in communication techniques and information retrieval. The money obtained from these contracts and courses will be used to pay teaching assistants.

CHAPTER EIGHT

Case study: Roskilde University Centre
User education in the framework of project studies

THE UNIVERSITY CENTRE at Roskilde, Denmark, was opened in 1972. It is one of a series of new universities experimenting with a type of educational pattern based on problem-orientated project studies.

This form of higher education is interesting in the context of library user education, partly because it implies specific ways of using the library as an information centre, partly because it brings out features of library use which are also found in connection with more traditional forms of higher education, but which are seldom recognised when the objectives and methods of library user education are formulated and discussed.

Project studies at the University Centre

At Roskilde University Centre, project work is integrated into the general educational pattern of the university. Students take part in a two year 'basic study' programme in the humanities, social sciences or natural sciences. After passing the final examination for this basic programme, students are accepted for further studies at the university, leading either to the equivalent of the master's degree, or to an intermediate degree level. After taking a master's degree, students may spend a further two to three years on a 'Licenciat' degree—equivalent to a PhD.

During the two-year basic studies programme, the student carries out a number of projects and also takes part in compulsory disciplinary and inter-disciplinary courses and foreign language courses. Throughout his/her time in the basic study programme, the student is part of a 'house' consisting of sixty to seventy students and five to six teachers. This 'house' is a physical as well as an organisational and social unit. In each, there are nine group rooms for six to eight students, five to six teachers' offices, a room for the secretary, a lecture room for up to thirty students, a lunch-room (with seating capacity for twenty persons) and facilities for the use of AV equipment and for copying.

The house teachers are collectively responsible for planning the two-year course of study for their house, within the framework outlined by the university authorities. The teachers work out introductory courses, certain other courses and suggestions for projects. They are also responsible for following the general progress of the students in the house and for individual guidance. Decisions concerning the whole of a house, the detailed planning of courses and evaluation as well as the progress of individual project groups are discussed at weekly or fortnightly house meetings.

The project studies included in the course of basic studies are based on an analysis of the types of complex problems of society that the students will meet later on in their working life. The projects require both theoretical insight and techniques embodied in several traditional subjects, so the approach has to be interdisciplinary. Students have to learn to plan and work in a group, and have, amongst other things, to learn to evaluate their plans and their work and progress.

At Roskilde, each project is planned and carried out by a small number of students (five to nine) together with one or more university teachers (professors, lecturers, or assistant lecturers), who act as tutors for their groups. There is a fixed time-limit for each project—usually one term. At the end of the set time, the students have to present a report on the work carried out. This report is usually examined and evaluated by both internal and external examiners.

Work on a project usually proceeds through the following phases:
1 The project is proposed either by the teachers or by the students, and an agreement is reached by the group of students and the teacher after a negotiation over the main trends in the project.
2 The students begin to acquire some background knowledge of the problem area and the theories and methods that might be useful in the treatment of the problem. This includes a search for literature on the subjects and an intensive consultation with the teachers.
3 A more specific problem is formulated and an investigation into this problem is outlined. Literature treating this more specific problem is searched.
4 The investigation is carried out. Plans are revised as the investigation develops and the students get more insight into the factual, theoretical, and methodological problems involved. The problem formulation may be revised as a result of new insights or theoretical and practical problems. The investigation may consist of the study of literary sources or it may involve experiments or interviews. In this phase, the students may search for more general treatments of the field to supplement their over-all understanding of the problem, they may search for source materials, or they may be looking for information about methods of investigation and an actual investigation to be used as a model.

5 The results of the investigation are recorded in a report. The report includes a discussion of the way the project has been conducted and documentation on the literature used.

6 The report is presented to the other students and other teachers for a thorough discussion and evaluation. This discussion usually takes three to five hours.

7 The group reviews the discussion and the evaluation and goes through the report again, summing up the results and shortcomings of the group as a guideline for future work. They may also change parts of the report, but seldom do so.

In order to make sure that the students have a broad understanding of the subject fields and the theories and methods involved in the projects, their studies can be supplemented by other activities such as courses and tutorials. Special skills such as language proficiency or the routines of the chemistry laboratory are taught in course form. However, since the projects are intended to form the dominant part of the education programme, these other activities can only take up a limited part of the time schedule of the student. At Roskilde, project work occupies at least half the students' time.

The basic studies programme in the humanities

Experience with user education has been limited to the basic studies programme in the humanities, and this will briefly be described. The basic studies programme centres upon the cultural institutions of society, including the family, socialisation and education, the complex character of popular culture, the mass media and the public etc, as well as the material and economic aspects of these institutions. Students are expected to try to work out a coherent conception of language and culture in their social context.

Through project-work, the students are introduced to the problems of scholarly and scientific work in theory and practice. Emphasis is placed on learning to communicate the results of project work to others, particularly people outside the student's own sphere of work. Students and teachers discuss the function of research in the humanities, in society, and—at least preliminarily—the problems of the work-situation in which students will find themselves at the end of the final examination.

The programme comprises the following theoretical and methodological areas or dimensions:

The philosophical dimension Philosophy and history of ideas. General methodology and theory of science with special regard to the humanities.

85

The dimension of textual and communicational studies Literary and linguistic studies. Mass media and general theories of the content and form of communication.

The historical-sociological dimension Theories and methods of history and sociology. Description of contemporary society and its historical development.

The pedagogical-psychological dimension Psychology, theories and practice of education, theory of socialisation and qualifications, cognitive theory and social psychology.

In order to guide the students through a programme that will enable them to acquire the experience, knowledge, and skills necessary for further studies at the university, a two-year framework is set up for each class of students. A theme for each of the first three terms is delineated; the fourth term does not have a theme. The themes serve as bases for project choice and for the coordination of courses and other activities during the term. Such themes may be: 'The form and content of communication', 'Socialisation and education', 'Mass media', 'The cultural institutions of society'. In introductory courses of two weeks at the beginning of each term, the respective themes are presented, with examples of appropriate theories and methods, by the teachers, together with suggestions for projects.

During the two-year basic studies programme, the student has to carry out four projects, of which one will have to treat either a historical problem (before 1945) or problems of culture and society of a foreign-language community (outside Scandianavia).

In addition to this, the student has to take part in four obligatory disciplinary and interdisciplinary courses on theories and methods taken from the four dimensions and four foreign-language courses.

The design and organisation of Roskilde University Library

The library at Roskilde University Centre has been designed to support the needs of the teachers and students in connection with, amongst other things, project work.

Library buildings

Roskilde University Library was planned as a decentralised library consisting of several departments spread throughout the campus, each containing books and periodicals pertaining to different subject areas. However, the transdisciplinary nature of the various projects led to a need for the students to visit several buildings in order to obtain the material necessary for their studies. This has led to a shift of opinion in favour of aiming at a centralised library though no detailed planning has yet been possible. Students are allowed to borrow most of the publications from the library and use them in their group rooms or at home.

Contents of the library collection

The university library purchases between one and twenty copies of each book according to demand. The most highly used have not been standard university textbooks, but comprehensive historical works, classics of economic history and theory, government publications of various types and statistical works.

What makes the problem of numbers of loan copies particularly important in the case of this university is the fact that all students are producing their projects under an immense time pressure which in many cases does not allow them to wait even one week for the book they need. They must either get hold of the book quickly or redefine their project so as to get around it; the latter solution tends to detract from the quality of the project. In this respect, it is possible for the library to contribute to a better quality of student work by acquiring several copies of much-used books.

Library service

Demands on library service—where service is taken to mean everything done by library staff to ease the students' search/finding of literature for their projects—differ considerably from corresponding demands at more traditional research libraries. Special effort has been made towards improvement of library services in three areas: a) the tools for information searching and retrieval produced by the library—such as the catalogues; b) the individual 'face-to-face' help given by the library staff to the students; c) the teaching of methods for literature searching.

a) Improvement of the tools for information retrieval

Classification systems of the hierarchical type such as UDC which is used at Roskilde are often difficult to use in connection with interdisciplinary problem-orientated work, because most projects cut across the hierarchical groupings of the classification system. At Roskilde University Library, work has been carried out on an alphabetical entry system, providing the students with an immediately comprehensible search entry point.

b) Individual help from librarians

This form of help often requires discussion between the librarian and the student in an attempt to analyse and define the exact nature of the information search. Search models have been worked out by the library staff as a help to getting students started on their searches. Face-to-face work of the type just described is very time-consuming and for this reason alone it is not feasible as the major type of improvment of the library's service.

c) Teaching of methods for literature searching

At Roskilde University, the development of methods for the teaching of literature searching has been given high priority, because this is considered to be of fundamental importance in connection with project-organised studies. This has resulted in changes in the role of the librarians and changes in the librarians' conceptions of their functions. At Roskilde there is much greater emphasis on the educational function of the librarians than at many of the traditional university libraries.

Approaches to the use of libraries and literature searching
a) Teachers

The task of the teachers in project-organised work is to help the project group solve the problem it has chosen; at the same time they are supposed to help the students to verbalise and generalise the processes they are involved in. This includes the literature search, where teachers must be able to help the students solve the immediate problem of their project-orientated search for the relevant literature and at the same time learn the general principles of literature searching.

At Roskilde, one or two teachers concurrently participate in the work of the project group. They have a general knowledge of the group's subject area, but not necessarily of the specific project problem. They are, to a large extent, involved in a process similar to that of the student members of the group. The success of the teaching depends partly on the extent to which the teachers and students are able to verbalise the development and interrelations of their cognitive processes.

How do teachers deal with the problem of teaching the techniques of literature searching?

1 The teachers may be subject specialists for the project subject and supply the students with all the necessary bibliographical information. The actual process of the literature search is hardly discussed at all.

2 The teachers carry out the literature search and hand over the results to the students without any comments on the search process. This may be due to a feeling of insecurity about the teacher's personal methods of literature searching. This again results in a situation where the students have little opportunity to discuss and define the formulation of their specific search information problem, and little chance of learning the general principles of information searching.

3 Teachers sometimes explain to students how they themselves have carried out the search. This method allows for discussion about the formulation of the problem, but gives the students a passive role.

4 Often students try to find the literature they require themselves, without any help from their teachers, who confine themselves to commenting on the results of the search. This involves the students in an active process but provides them with little help with regard to discovering general methods for systematic literature searching.

5 Students may be provided, in advance, with general guidelines, and then allowed to carry out the search themselves. This only occurs in

a few instances probably because it is a rather difficult task, especially for a teacher not accustomed to planning a systematic search.

6 The ideal case is where both students and teachers actively engage in the search. This method, too, is rarely used. It requires a certain amount of knowledge of, and training in, systematic information searching on the part of the teachers and an ability to communicate this to other people. Its advantages lie in the fact that the teachers always have a chance to explain mistakes and propose alternative strategies and in this way prevent disappointments from becoming too dominant and demotivating.

b) Students

The first year at university represents a time of considerable psycho-social adjustment and cognitive restructuring for all students, regardless of age or background. At Roskilde, students are presented with a much broader range of choices than those experienced during their school-days. For example, at school it is usually the teachers who suggest what students should read and students only rarely are expected to find literature on their own. In the basic studies programme, they are confronted with a much wider choice of types of material—textbooks, encyclopedias, periodicals, reports, government publications and so on, and the choice of the literature to use is in the hands of the group.

Students, during the first and even into the second terms continue to find their literature much in the same way as they have done at school. The students usually ask the question 'Do you have anything on topic x?' of the librarians. They go directly to the shelves and pick up anything that seems to be of interest. Readability of books and general opinion of authors are the main criteria new students use for the evaluation of titles found in the public libraries and book shops. Most students continue to use the public libraries to a considerable extent throughout their basic studies programme, but the university library is used with sharply increasing frequency from the second term onwards, though not very much for inter-library loans which are usually effected through the local public library.

Students increasingly experience the finding of literature as a problem. They become aware that they have to search in several places in order to find material on a given topic. The criteria for choice change in the direction of greater discrimination. Communication patterns with librarians change—students no longer ask for 'something'—they provide additional information on the purpose and time-limitations of their search and try to find out 'what' is available. Students appear to become gradually better at locating literature themselves and communicating their needs to librarians, but they do not in any way experience the librarians as agents of control. They rely heavily on the judgement of their teachers with regard to the most important literature for their projects. The students realise that only certain kinds of literature on a given subject will be acceptable to their teachers or examiners. Rarely do project groups base their work on publications which their teachers have not at least accepted. This type of reliance on teachers does not contribute to the students' insight into the strategies for literature searching. In those cases where teachers do not motivate their choices, students demand reasons and specifications, but they hardly ever ask where, and they never ask how, teachers find the literature they recommend—and teachers do not usually volunteer such information.

A course in literature searching and library use
for humanities students at Roskilde University Centre

Against the background of problem-orientated project studies described above, it was decided, in 1974, to develop a course on elementary research methodology. This was specifically aimed at supporting project work. The five modules of the course devised corresponded roughly to major processes in the development of a project: problem formulation, literature search, argumentation, documentation, and report writing. Since 1975 a team of three teachers and a librarian have spent considerable time on investigating problems relating to the literature search. A number of general principles have evolved, from experience with project work, from theoretical and empirical studies in linguistics, epistemology, methodology, education, and the social dynamics of research groups. These principles have guided the planning and teaching of courses on literature searching.

After what has been said so far, it will hardly be surprising that the literature search is not taught as a set of techniques or directions such as found in a cookery book. This would be in direct contrast to the nature of project work. Since the course aims at strengthening awareness of continuity and mutual influence between work on a problem and literature search as one of several research methods, special attention has been paid to the following aspects:

1 Timing and duration

Since the first term is a time for considerable psycho-social adjustment and restructuring of the cognitive processes, it was decided to place the course after that time. At present, the course is given during the third or fourth term, when there are fewer obligatory courses.

Students are given a brief introduction to the library by library personnel, during the first term.

The course on literature searching consists of twelve hours, grouped into four sessions. This is supplemented by continuous practical work and experience of literature searching, in connection with projects.

The course begins directly after the student groups have begun their work on preliminary problem formulations. The teaching group continues to follow the development of the projects and is not just interested in the fact that the students have found some literature but also in how they have found it, what they have eliminated on what grounds, and how they work with the literature. Since most of the group are teachers, this does not present the same problems that it would for librarians. In the fourth session, towards the end of the term, the group works with the students on the setting up of references, citations, and bibliographies.

2 Participants

In order to achieve a connection between the literature search course and other studies, the literature search courses are held within the framework of one term's theme, preferably for one house where each class consists of two to four project groups. Students register for the literature search course at the beginning of term, in their respective project groups. Classes of fifteen to twenty-two students are formed by the course teachers on the basis of student suggestions and of the suitability of various combinations of subjects.

3 Teacher resources

The initial teacher/student ratio was high, and this led to difficulties as demands for the courses rose. Teaching material has now been prepared which enables a reduction in the teacher/student ratio and allows the courses to be transferred to other groups.

4 Materials

Written and oral information on the content of the course and on out-of-course work is given to the students at the following points— before registration for the course, at the beginning of the course and at the beginning of each session.

A loose-leaf textbook or manual has been prepared for these courses. The first chapter describes several ways in which different people— students, teachers, research workers—actually carry out literature searches via individual contacts, following up of footnotes and bibliographies in publications ('chain-searching') and systematic bibliographic searching. The advantages and disadvantages of each of these methods are discussed. Students are asked to read this chapter before the beginning of the course.

During the course, students are given several authors' descriptions of literature search processes as part of their work on a problem. Other handouts include information on the university library and its personnel, on the searching of legal and statistical information, and on types of questions that can be answered by different types of bibliographies.

All students are familiarised with and practise using dictionaries, thesauri, and encyclopedias. The book catalogues of the university library (alphabetic and systematic), the classification scheme used by the Danish public libraries, a few abstract publications, and guides to libraries in Denmark, are used by all students.

5 Course content

The course content briefly is:

Session one. Literature search as related to problem formulation: forms of literature search; search terms and the use of dictionaries, thesauri and encyclopedias.

Session two. Making use of local university library resources on the basis of search terms: use of alphabetic catalogues, exercises exemplifying typical problems; introduction to classification systems; use of the systematic catalogues with the help of the group's search terms; problems of relevance and precision.

Session three. Selection of search tools organised on the basis of criteria of: subject field/discipline/topic; period; language and nationality; publication media; making use of other libraries and of the interlibrary loan; problems of co-ordination of searches.

Session four. Personal documentation, citation, the writing of references and the arrangement of bibliographies.

6 Location

The first and fourth sessions are held in the students' respective 'houses', sessions two and three at the university library.

Epistemological and pedagogical aspects

One of the main aims for these courses has been to bring about greater insight on the part of the students—and possibly their teachers— into the relationships between literature search and research methodology. Project-organised studies have been regarded as a form of 'learning by researching', which aims at an ever increasing awareness on the part of the students of different types of problems and different approaches to their clarification or solution. It is suggested that learning by researching provides students with increased possibilities for learning through making and correcting their own mistakes, and through thinking about their own successes and failures.

A mere accumulation of data gathered in, for example field work, case studies, content analysis etc does not qualify as learning by researching. This requires investigations of types of assumptions, postulates, hypotheses, theories and of the interrelations between them, and also how and in which social context different groups, schools and traditions arrive at certain statements. The course designers found it necessary to delineate several approaches to a problem, to develop the students' awareness of the influence of search strategies and tools on the literature found and thereby on the problem formulation. Students were asked to develop and explain their various choices throughout the courses.

In any form of learning/teaching situation there is some form of balance between general and specific aims. In course-based studies there is a constant tension between the general aims of a curriculum (though those might not even be clearly specified) and the courses placed into it. What students attend and what they pay attention to is frequently determined by examination regulations. Aside from the fact that curricula limit choices, students themselves economise with their time and other resources. Under pressure from various sides, students can lose sight of the general aims of a curriculum and take the general to be that which is relevant for examinations. The specific are illustrative examples, exercises, and 'sidelines' pursued by teachers. In such studies, students frequently become impatient with, and have little use for, perspectives not related to examination questions, even when they touch on broader issues or issues of their professional practice-to-be. The fact that student knowledge has a tendency to become encyclopedic has resulted in various forms of curriculum planning and integration, emphasis on general method courses and the like. However, such integration necessarily entails the co-operation of teachers—collective planning, team teaching—which has been rather difficult to implement at most universities.

In project studies such as at Roskilde, the problem takes on a different form. For one thing, the general frameworks meant that teachers have had to learn to plan collectively, to teach in teams, to relate the contents of courses to each other and to projects. This learning process of teachers has not been easy, but at least in the humanities department it has resulted in fairly well-established relationships of cooperation amongst teachers within a house and across house boundaries. In this way, students do not acquire unrelated, encyclopedic knowledge. However, the tension between the general and the specific remains. Students have a tendency to become deeply engrossed on the project they are working on—which also serves as a basis for evaluation and examinations. They tend to have little use for obligatory courses in theory and methodology aiming at the broadening of the contexts of individual projects.

The planning of courses on research methodology and on literature search, has tried to relate them as far as possible to the respective term themes, to other courses attended by the students, and to individual projects. They have been designed so that they provide opportunities for the students to reflect upon previous and present practice.

The following form has been aimed at:

1 General orientation, presentation of the general theme and/or general principles.

2 Exemplification by the teachers by means of: a) special *types* of questions, topics, problem areas, applications; b) *specific* solutions described by others.

3 Exemplification by the students by means of their project based searches.

4 Comparison and generalisation of results of the project groups' work in a plenary session.

Terminology: a process of development

The development and use of language is important in project-orientated studies in two ways. On the one hand the development of a student's vocabulary system parallels and enforces the development of cognitive structure. On the other hand a successful literature search is based on the imaginative use of everyday terms and scientific vocabulary. These two processes are closely related. During their studies, students work actively with their vocabulary systems, constantly writing down and discussing their understanding of the problem at hand, and the theories and methods they find adequate. This activity indirectly helps them during their literature search. Conversely, work with terminology during a literature search may help to develop understanding of the problem being tackled.

The development and structuring of terminology occurs to a large extent during the problem formulation phase. A problem is discussed, analysed and formulated with increasing precision. The literature search usually starts with this process of analysis and definition, and the research team in Roskilde have pointed out that the search can be utilised to develop the semantic sensibility of the group and to encourage students to distinguish keenly between different semantic, terminological structures. The literature search should keep the project group together as a teaching unit, so as not to interrupt the group process. In addition, the search should 'point out how it is possible to find one's way among competing theories and methods by means of the accessible bibliographical resources'.

Instruction in the use of bibliographical tools

In many cases, advanced user instruction is more or less the same as instruction in subject bibliography. This is an indication of the importance that has been attached to the use of these tools by the course designers—usually librarians.

The research team in Roskilde believe that this area of literature search has been grossly over-emphasised, and in fact has been the cause of failure in many user instruction programmes. It is extremely important that in teaching students to search literature, the bibliographical search is viewed and presented as only one of many types of work patterns.

In the course in literature searching and library use for the humanities students at Roskilde, the use of bibliographies is introduced rather late in the course and takes up comparatively little time. The use of bibliographies is introduced during the third three-hour session of the course and approximately two hours, out of the total twelve, are devoted to this topic. The aim is to get students to analyse their own project search problems and decide whether they require to carry out a systematic bibliographical search, and, if so, which type of tool they will need to use. It is not intended to teach the students how to use a number of specific bibliographies, but to make them aware of the existence of this type of tool and the situations in which bibliographies can be useful.

The method used to train the students to recognise the context in which a bibliography might be a good tool, is by the demonstration of three types of delimitations of project themes which point to different bibliographical solutions: a) delimitation of the subject with respect to subject fields/topics; b) a temporal delimitation; and c) a geographical/linguistic delimitation.

With respect to the first type of delimitation, the students are presented with some information on the common divisions or classifications of subjects which are generally reflected in the structure of subject bibliographies. This leads to a discussion of the problems of using subject-orientated bibliographies in connection with projects which are basically interdisciplinary, and this discussion constitutes the focal point of this type of delimitation. Apart from this, some of the weaknesses of bibliographical tools are illustrated; for instance, the fact that in most cases it is very difficult to search on anything but the *topic* of the publication, whereas the methods and theories of the publications are not used as entries.

The temporal delimitation of the project theme involves an analysis, carried out by the students, to explicate how the content of their project necessitates a search in the literature production of a particular period. If, for instance, a project group intends to analyse 'Public debate on atomic energy', they will have to make an assessment as to the period in which this debate has taken place, and this will vary with respect to the country in question. This will give them a temporal frame within which to conduct their literature search.

Also in this connection, the students are shown problems of searching literature for projects dealing with very recent events or very newly defined disciplines, ie the built-in time lag in the publication of periodicals and books is illustrated.

The third type of delimitation, the geographical and linguistic one, serves two purposes. First, it helps the students to evaluate, at an early stage in their project, whether problems with the language of the project literature will prevent them from doing qualified work on the topic chosen. For instance, a group of Danish students doing a project on, say, 'Migration of labour in southern Italy' will most likely run into a linguistic problem, because not much literature about this very specific problem is likely to have been translated into major European languages. And secondly, the purpose of the geographical/linguistic delimitation is to teach the students to recognise search situations in which the use of national bibliographies rather than subject bibliographies might be of use.

After these demonstrations, the students are asked to analyse their own projects in the same manner, in order to decide for themselves when and how to use subject bibliographies in their own search. This approach springs from a scepticism regarding the omnipotence of the bibliographical apparatus, and from a conception of the student as someone whose major need is to *learn how to choose his tools intelligently.*

Conclusions

The main goals of the course in literature searching and library use for the humanities students at Roskilde University Centre have been concerned with improving the students' capacities for planning and carrying out a search—how and where to begin—and with the evaluation of the searches and the literature found. In addition the students have been trained in specific skills in the use of various tools for locating literature. The course is designed to help the students to become increasingly independent in their work, particularly problem-orientated project studies.

It has been suggested that it is of prime importance to integrate the teaching of literature and information searching into the general study pattern of the students. At Roskilde, students in the humanities are now required to analyse and document their literature search processes in connection with each project and to discuss them during both internal evaluations and external examinations. Teaching material has been developed to assist in this process. This material may also serve to teach the teachers the process involved in literature searching.

CHAPTER NINE

User education in the United Kingdom

THERE IS a widespread belief amongst librarians in the UK that it is necessary for students to be trained or instructed in the use of libraries and literature. Although many librarians have long regarded user education as beneficial, not until the last five to ten years has any marked effort been put into the establishment and development of programmes, which are now seen to be an essential component of a library's overall operation. The historical development of the field in the UK can be traced in articles by Tidmarsh and Mews. It is not intended that this chapter should retrace that history but rather illuminate the problems faced in user education by describing the present state-of-the-art.

At the present time nearly all universities and polytechnics in the UK provide some form of user education. It is not possible to describe what is being done in each institution, and the variation of approach from one institution to another, and from one course to another makes it possible to give only an overview of the present scene. The material for this overview was collected in 1975 and from published sources both before and since that date. Since user education is a constantly changing and developing field it may well be that some of the information about individual institutions is no longer correct. This should not, however, seriously affect the overall picture presented.

Though a set of aims and objectives for a user education programme would enable the expected outcome of the programme to be stated, very few libraries have specified their aims. The expressed or implied aim appears to be, in general terms, to enable the student to achieve maximum utilisation of library resources and services. Programmes established to achieve this aim are usually in two stages.

Orientation

Orientation is concerned with introducing the user to the general techniques of library usage and services available in libraries and, in particular, to the organisation, services, and layout of one particular library. This general introduction to libraries is felt to be essential because

97

the use of libraries is seldom taught in schools. New students usually do not understand how to use libraries. Provision at this stage in the programme varies considerably from institution to institution depending on the local situation particularly with regard to the organisation of freshers', induction, or pre-sessional weeks or their equivalents. There is no common pattern. However, it is apparent that the smaller the institution or library, the more personalised the introduction becomes and the more effective it is thought to be. Most libraries are not in a position, much as they would wish to be, to give personal help of this kind and have to use other approaches. These can be arranged according to the timing of the orientation programme.

Induction programmes

Many libraries use the opportunity of an organised pre-sessional programme for new students to introduce the library to new users, usually in their first few days at the institution. Librarians are becoming increasingly aware that the first few days of a student's contact with the library should be concerned with affective objectives, ie the creation of attitudes rather than the imparting of information. In other words, contact at this time should be inspirational.

Methods that are adopted include lectures or talks by the librarian, usually to large groups; talks by senior staff or subject specialists; guided tours (though these are losing popularity because of the physical constraints associated with their organisation), tape/slide or film introductions to the library and the distribution of printed library guides. These methods are used alone or in any combination according to the taste of those responsible for organising the session. For example, students at Cranfield Institute of Technology are addressed for forty-five minutes on their second day by the librarian, whereas at St Mary's Hospital Medical School a clear, detailed guide to the library is preferred to talks and tours. The length of time allocated also varies considerably, eg ten to fifteen minute tours at Dundee University; 1½ hours at Lanchester Polytechnic, consisting of a twenty minute tape/slide programme followed by a talk and discussion and then a tour of the library.

Most institutions follow a standard pattern for all departments or student groups, though at Bath University the use made of the one hour given to the library in the school orientation courses is left to the discretion of the relevant information officer. Whatever the format adopted, the content is generally similar. This includes the library's collections, services and internal arrangement, location of material in special collections or for a particular subject, borrowing procedures, the catalogue, etc, and, more particularly, creating the impression that the library is a place where help is available and that the library staff are helpful and friendly.

The tape/slide package is the most popular audio-visual aid used to convey this information and message. It is usually used in conjunction with a talk or tour, and has been widely adopted because it eliminates the necessity for the library staff to repeat the same material again and again. Tape/slides used in orientation sessions are very similar in content. The length and the depth of coverage of specific aspects may vary, but the approach and contents are uniform. Exceptions are Hull University, where, though traditional in approach, the commentary is amusing but not patronising, and Sussex University. Here *Using the university library* is a tape/slide cartoon designed to stimulate new users to think about the role of the library in their education and the way in which librarian and user interact. There is little if any informational content to the package.

Of the other media, film is used at Aberdeen University, where a twenty minute introduction is shown to groups as part of their tour of the campus. Tours of the library are available at a later stage for those who wish to make use of them. Videotape is used by Brunel University, and by Salford University where it supplements a five-minute talk by the librarian to new students. Nottingham University is moving to videotape from tape/slide for the introduction to the library. This is shown in the main building of the university in the first week of the new session and in the library foyer in the second. It should be pointed out, however, that there is a move away from audio-visual aids. Bath University, for example, has tried both videotape and tape/slide and no longer uses either.

Follow-up sessions

The time available in this early contact with new users is mainly used for inspirational purposes. The main message is that the library has a major role to play in the student's education and that the library staff are available to help. Several libraries endeavour to follow the inspirational message of the first few days with a more informative session at a later stage. For example, students in the Faculty of Commerce and Social Science at Birmingham University are shown a tape/slide introduction to the library and are taken on a tour of the building during Freshers' Week. They return in small groups in the fourth and fifth weeks of their first term for an hour long practical session on locating material on reading lists. At Southampton University, 200-300 engineering and science students attend a forty-five minute lecture in their second week, having received a five to ten minute talk by the librarian and seen a ten minute tape/slide in their first week. Often the initial introduction to the library is a little impersonal and so departmental talks and tours of small groups are arranged at a later stage in the first term. At Sheffield Polytechnic the librarian talks to 1500 new students in the first week and departmental talks and tours are arranged later for groups of fifteen to twenty.

Polytechnic libraries seem to have been more successful in extending their orientation programmes in this way. Many follow the first week introductions with courses of up to eight hours spread over the first term. Plymouth Polytechnic for example, follows the one-hour introductory unit with six hours more detailed introduction to the Learning Resource Centre, sources of information and study techniques. Practical work is also included.

The philosophy behind these follow-up sessions is that only when a student has met problems in literature use will he see the relevance of library instruction. Most students do not meet these problems during their first week at university. For this reason some libraries organise their introductory sessions later in the term rather than during the first few days. However, timetabling difficulties may still mean that the sessions are held in the first two weeks or so, as at Loughborough University. Here students in small departmental groups receive a 'seminar on location' tour of the library.

Guides and guiding

Almost all libraries produce printed guides to the library which are distributed as part of the orientation programme. The variations in content and format are considerable, reflecting to some degree the different attitudes of librarians to their usefulness. Many are produced because they always have been; others are an act of faith produced in the belief that they are not read or used but in the hope that they will be. There is a trend towards a more concise, often pocket-size, booklet or A4 sheets folded in a variety of ways. As well as the general library guides, there are also guides to specific departmental libraries, guides to the library for specific groups of students, guides to catalogue use, bookmarks, and guides in the form of collections of leaflets about individual services of the library.

One reason why library guides are produced is to enable the reader to find his own way around the library. One other way of providing this self-help is the provision of adequate guiding or signposting in the library. Some librarians feel that the only reason tours are included in orientation sessions is to compensate for inadequate guiding. Others make the point that if the important information is available at the point of need in the form of good guiding, then library guides become redundant. Certainly good guiding is thought to be more valuable than a good library guide. So important a role does guiding appear to play, that several librarians state that library instruction becomes almost impossible without it.

Postgraduate students and academic staff

Most of this section on orientation has related to the provision of programmes for undergraduate students or students new to higher education establishments. New postgraduate students and new members of staff seem to receive less consideration. Usually the needs of post-graduates, which differ from those of undergraduates, are nevertheless met in the same way, though there are exceptions. For example, individual tours are given to arts postgraduates at Durham University. Postgraduates at polytechnics tend to be few in number and they receive more individual treatment. Treatment for new staff is often very informal with ad hoc arrangements being made. At Hull University, personal tours are arranged by subject specialists as part of the induction week for new staff organised by the university. A guide—*The university's library*, is specially produced for staff. Similar arrangements are made at Loughborough University.

Bibliographic instruction

Nearly all university and polytechnic libraries progress further than the orientation stage by providing as a second stage in their user education programme courses of bibliographic instruction. Again the variation of approach from one institution to another is such that no illuminative collective experience can be presented. The differing views expressed on the different problems affecting user education can be summarised as follows.

Course organisation

As so much of course organisation depends on the individuals involved, there is a great variety of approaches. Both formal and informal methods are used to organise courses, though in most institutions a mixture of the two is used. Formal methods of approach include invitations to academic staff via the library guide or circular letters to consider instructional courses for their students. Hull University Library invites all postgraduates by letter to attend a library instruction course. Letters of encouragement are also sent to supervisors and heads of departments. At Southampton University all undergraduates receive a letter containing the timetable and outline for a course which they are invited to attend.

The most important method used, however, to organise courses is personal contact. This may also be semi-formal, as at Exeter University where the librarian phones all the deans of faculties to invite their co-operation, but usually the approach is informal. Librarians build up personal contacts in a number of ways; through acquisitions contacts, through library liaison representatives, by attendance at departmental meetings or boards of studies etc. It appears that those libraries with greatest impact in user education are those where librarians are active members of the institution. It is worth noting that the smaller and more closely knit the unit in which the librarian operates, the easier it is to develop personal relationships which can lead to the acceptance of courses.

101

The timing of user education programmes has to be agreed between the library and the academic departments. Experience suggests that student motivation is highest immediately prior to embarking on a dissertation, project or literature search. However the experience of Loughborough University, where courses are held in the first year, suggests that this need not be the case. In any event, whatever the merits of particular times, the limiting factor appears to be when the department is prepared to make time available. A great deal depends on the conviction of course tutors etc of the value of the user education programme. There is a temptation to use user education as a course filler for example between examinations and the end of term, when it has no obvious relevance, or relationship, to the rest of the academic course. Bristol and Hull universities seem, however, to use this period to good effect. The question of timing is less important for postgraduate courses, but they too are likely to be most effective if given at the moment of need.

On the question of how much time should be allocated to user education opinion varies widely between those who suggest restricting instruction to what is needed for the particular course in question, and those who have a packaged programme to be used in all situations. Courses in the same subject field could, therefore, vary from one to two hours up to fifteen to twenty hours depending on the institution giving the course. Despite the fact that several librarians suggest the optimum course duration to be four to six hours, there is no evidence to suggest that one course length is more effective than any other. The limiting factor is usually not what is best, but what is possible within the departmental timetable.

One other factor which could affect timetabling of courses, is the size of the group. Trent Polytechnic, for example, limits the size of groups for library instruction courses to six. For a large department, therefore, several timetable slots have to be found. Generally the departmental group becomes the user education group and this has implications on where the instruction takes place. Though large groups are the norm in practice (usually upwards of twelve to fifteen), most librarians would prefer, if not individual tuition, groups of no more than eight.

Although it is assumed that all members of an institution are equally in need of instruction, the majority of courses noted in the survey were provided for science, technology and engineering undergraduates. One reason given for this is that science and engineering students are more used to receiving information in courses and lectures. Although the difference in the number of courses organised for science, as opposed to arts, students is marked, that between courses for undergraduates, as opposed to postgraduates, is very large indeed. Only Hull and Sheffield universities seem to be doing more for postgraduates than for under-graduates, and many institutions make no provision for postgraduates at all. No reasons for this division are apparent.

Course content

It is almost impossible to consider the content of an 'average' course, not least because the structure of courses varies so greatly. The most common approach to bibliographic instruction is to base the format on the NLL (BLLD) pattern of a literature search and so work systema-tically through the different sources of information and their use. This format usually includes definition of the subject, finding an introduction to the subject, locating reviews and bibliographies, tracing journal articles (information explosion and the need for secondary literature could be introduced here), current awareness, other sources of information (theses, reports, etc) and locating relevant people and institutions. Citation practice, personal indexes, report writing and computerised information services are introduced at appropriate points in the discus-sion. Even where this particular pattern is not used, a survey of the different types of information source and literature formats is common.

The case study method, where a literature search on a particular topic is used to illustrate principles, is not widely used. In some cases it is because the librarian believes that this approach often omits im-portant reference works, ie all material, which would be included in a systematic approach, would not necessarily be included in the case study. Others disagree and find the approach quite attractive. However, since a fresh case study is required for each course, time considerations often prevent its use. Other approaches include the common-package and the problem-centred course. The latter is based on the type of query that the student might have to face. Sources are introduced in so far as they relate to the query under discussion. An extension of the problem-centred method involves individual tuition. It is based on the thesis that real 'teaching' is only possible when the individual has a specific problem and makes an individual approach for assistance. This individual approach is very labour-intensive and so, although it is favoured by many, it is not always practical. One way of overcoming this problem favoured by several libraries, is to continue with the formal courses which reach greater numbers of people and then to provide a follow-up service by being available to individuals who require clarification or further help. The manner in which this follow-up service is provided is very varied. In many libraries, enquiry desks only deal with simple routine queries and transfer anything of a more complex nature to subject specialists or information staff. In others, readers' enquiry or advisory desks are manned by senior staff on a rota basis. Alternatively, many libraries have reading room enquiry points which are manned by information officers, or the subject specialists, rather than one central reference point. Individual tutorials depend on human-to-human contact. The impersonal approach to individual teaching, programmed or computer-aided instruction, does not appear to be used in any library instruction programmes in the UK.

An increasing number of libraries are including practical work, not only in bibliographic instruction but also in orientation programmes, as part of the course. Students learn by doing, not by being told. Library and information use is a practical skill acquired through practice not teaching, and more and more librarians are beginning to recognise that some form of practical work as part of, or linked to, their courses is essential. Projects can be designed to give the student a better knowledge of the way to use the library, its catalogues and services or to give him experience of using the literature. In either case the librarian has to convince the student of the value of the exercise. Projects designed by the librarian alone, especially projects on the use of the catalogue, are often treated flippantly and regarded as irrelevant by the student. Exercises designed by librarians and academic staff jointly to provide subject relevance also need 'selling' to the students, and apparently the easiest way to do this is to give some form of mark or assessment to the project which counts in the departmental assessment. Relevance then becomes clearer and motivation is increased, that is if attendance figures at courses are any guide. The obvious problem is that the librarian has to convince his academic colleagues not only of the need for providing a course of instruction, but also of the need for his cooperation in setting and marking projects. It appears that this is easier to do with science and engineering teachers than with arts and social science teachers.

The compilation of questions and topics demands considerable effort on the part of the librarian, especially if each student is to be given an individual set of questions or a unique topic for a search. Validating the questions and checking the problems that may be encountered in finding the answers also takes time. Considerable time is involved in supervising the students while they are undertaking the project or at least being available to help with queries if they arise. At the end of the project is the marking, checking and annotating of the completed project ready for return to the student in the shortest possible time. The whole exercise can be a very time-consuming, labour intensive operation and it is for this reason that many libraries, though agreeing with the rationale behind the inclusion of practical work, are unable to include it in courses. Those who consider it to be essential and have included it, have found it of great benefit.

Teaching facilities

As practical work comes to play a more important role both in orientation and instruction, the need for the library to have teaching

104

facilities of its own, close to the material under discussion, becomes more important. Very few libraries have no seminar or lecture rooms of any kind within the library building. The size of rooms available varies enormously from six-seat tutorial rooms to 100-seat lecture rooms. However some of those libraries with intermediate sized rooms seating twenty to thirty have insufficient space for some of the larger groups and departmental lecture theatres have to be used. Nearly all the seminar/lecture rooms contain provision for the use of audio-visual aids. Projection facilities for slides, OHP transparencies and film, together with television playback, plus the usual blackboard or whiteboard are provided in many of the rooms or are easily available. It might, therefore, be appropriate to consider which of these teaching aids are used and how.

Teaching aids

The most common teaching aid used in library instruction is chalk (and blackboard) supported by OHP transparencies for illustration. Slides are used as alternatives to transparencies at some libraries, notably Aston University which has a collection of 600 slides of the library, reference sources, abstracting and indexing services etc. Videotape is also used, but in very few libraries. Bradford University has produced its own videotape on how to use the catalogue and also uses the UMIST-prepared videotape on how to use abstracting and indexing services. Bradford University uses tape/slides for the case study literature searches, so the use of videotape introduces a different approach. Of the mixed media, tape/slide is the most commonly used because of its low cost and the familiarity that librarians now have with it. Librarians prefer to make their own tape/slides, rather than use those produced under the SCONUL scheme, for both teaching programmes and orientation courses. The main reason for this is that home-produced tape/slides are more relevant. SCONUL tape/slides are bought by a fair number of libraries, particularly the polytechnic libraries, and made available to readers, together with the home-made programmes, for self-instruction. It appears that audio-visual aids are not replacing personal contact with readers. Audio-visual aids are used as supplementary, not primary, materials.

Another major teaching aid is the handout. Designed with a specific local purpose in mind, these are the notes of the lecture and the continuing guidance that the student requires. Since handouts serve specific needs they vary from teacher to teacher. Even within one library the variety in range and depth of coverage of handouts can be quite substantial, and to attempt to describe them is impossible. In addition to the handouts given out as part of the course, most libraries also produce literature guides of a more permanent nature for the information of readers in general. Although these may be useful in teaching programmes, they are usually produced as teaching aids in their own right. They fall into six broad general classes. Firstly, there are guides to specific sources, eg *Guide to Chemical abstracts*, which attempt to explain the use of these specific sources with illustrative material and examples. The second class of guide deals with a specific subject field. Within this class these are several sub-classes. *Materials science—a guide to information in the library* produced by the University of Bath, is a printed twenty-eight page, A5 booklet, which overviews the types of material available. In contrast, *Ultrasonics—a guide to information in the library* also produced by Bath, is a single A4 sheet very similar to the *Pathfinders* of Project Intrex. This type of guide is popular, especially for the exploitation of subject material available in the library. There is a danger, mentioned by a handful of librarians, that unless care is taken, this type of guide can turn into a prestige publication first and a helpful guide second. The third class of guide includes leaflets and booklets designed to help the reader with technical points such as reference citation, bibliography compilation, literature search method and report writing. *Ideal author—notes on writing and presentation of research papers* produced by York University is typical of this type of guide. Lists of specific types of material make up the fourth class. Often these are produced in keyword listings as for example in the Newcastle University publication *Abstracting and indexing services in the university library*. Descriptions of classes of materials make up the fifth group; a good example is the *Readers' handbook* series produced by Hull University in A5 booklet format. Titles in the series include *British government publications, Periodicals* and *The Map Collection*. The final grouping, bookmarks with useful classmarks printed on them, has been mentioned earlier in connection with orientation.

Although similar types of publication are produced by many libraries, the degree of descriptive comment and other annotation included, varies. An obvious variation is in the format and style of the publications. Most libraries have tried to develop a house style for their publications to give a more professional and attractive appearance.

Evaluation

This is the area of user education described by Martyn as that 'area rich in speculation but uncommonly poor in demonstrable fact'. Instruction is usually provided on intuitition alone, a failing that could be avoided by purposeful evaluation and feedback. Librarians seem to assume that evaluation is a formal process, always involving pre- and post- tests or control groups. Evaluation can be defined as a systematic gathering together for analysis of information about what is taught and what is learned. Very little evaluation in this sense takes place, though many people collect subjective information by way of informal feedback.

This feedback comes from course committees, course tutors and project supervisors. The fact that there is a continuing demand in informal conversations for courses to continue or expand is often taken as a sign of approval and encouragement. Though this form of feedback is encouraging it is not very helpful in aiding the librarian to improve the courses given. Students and staff are normally too polite and not sufficiently constructively critical.

Librarians involved in setting and marking practical exercises as part of their courses are able to assess the effectiveness of the course by the way that the students perform on the practical work. Librarians not involved in this way are able to informally observe student use of the library, and to gain a subjective impression of the impact made by courses by noting the questions subsequently asked by students at the enquiry desk. A more formal approach is to elicit student reaction to courses by a questionnaire. Plymouth Polytechnic uses a questionnaire, which students complete anonymously, to find out how effective the teaching programme is and how relevant it is to students' needs. One section deals with the previous experience of the student in using libraries and information sources and this is the only reported case of establishing prior knowledge. Information about the habits and experience of students in using libraries is invaluable when planning courses designed to meet students' needs. The questionnaire continues by seeking the student's assessment of the course of lectures. Further comments on the points raised by the questions are invited, as are comments on the course as a whole. Suggestions for topics for inclusion in, or deletion from, the course are also sought.

Surrey University have also sought student views on library instruction courses. Students completed questionnaires at the conclusion of a course. They were asked how much of the information imparted was new, how useful they thought it would be, how much of the information might be picked up in other ways, their impression of the level of the course, why they had attended the course and whether they would favour the inclusion of a practical exercise as part of the course. The most frequent comment was that the courses should be as practical as possible and that the course should be appropriate to the student's need at that particular point in his course. The majority favoured the inclusion of a practical exercise. Final year students would have preferred the information earlier in their course.

Bradford University also uses questionnaires to assess the effectiveness of library seminars in the engineering courses. Students are asked whether the seminar achieved stated objectives. Further questions deal with specific components of the seminar and the student's assessment of them and of the overall programme. However, because the librarian responsible feels that evaluation is an integral part of the teaching process, he has begun to use criterion tests to measure the effectiveness of the teaching programme and to ascertain whether it is achieving its aims. Multiple-choice questions are used pre- and post- library instruction.

The questions have not been validated and could be biased towards the instruction being given. Nevertheless, this library has begun to take seriously the question of evaluation. Many more would do so if they received guidance on how to proceed. Others need convincing of the value of evaluation.

Course descriptions

It is instructive to consider descriptions of a few typical and not so typical user education programmes to highlight some of the points discussed above. Descriptions of other courses are to be found in the librarianship literature and some of the more recent ones are represented in the bibliography at the end of the book.

Plymouth Polytechnic Learning Resource Centre

The instruction programme at Plymouth Polytechnic has expanded rapidly since 1972 when a full time member of the LRC staff was appointed specifically for instructional purposes. Two further information officer appointments followed in 1973 and 1974. The aim of the programme is to reach every student, lecturer, and research assistant. Instruction is designed to match the needs of students at the various levels and stages of their studies and there is close cooperation with course tutors to achieve this. The programme for degree course students is based on three modules:

a) One hour induction/orientation—timed as early as possible in term one, preferably during the main induction at school level (module one).

b) Six hours introduction in term one to study techniques, LRC services, media, types of publication, etc (module two).

c) Twelve hours—bibliographical approach to project work, types and use of bibliographical tools, systematic literature searching, etc. Timed to coincide with the start of the project work in year two or three (module three).

Students on short courses usually receive a modified version of module one and HND students receive modules one and two. Modules one and two are given within complementary/general/liberal studies time and hence reach most full-time students. Module three usually forms part of timetabled course time, often necessitating a lecturer to give up lecture time. Module three is made up of eight elements, the first two of which are common to all subjects. All others are tailored to the group being taught:

Element 1: Review of previous LRC instruction—one hour.

       2: An approach to project work—choosing subject; preparation of bibliography; annotations; writing up; format—one hour.

       3: Bibliographies and indexing journals—definitions; scope and limitations; method of use—1½ hours.

   *4: Supervised search using indexing journals—two hours.

       5: Abstracting journals—definitions; scope and limitations; method of use—two hours.

   *6: Supervised search using abstracting journals—two hours.

       7: Citation indexes—1½ hours.

       8: Seminar and discussion—one hour.

*Wherever practical on the topic of the student's project.

Supplementary tutorials are organised for those students who wish to expand the knowledge gained as a result of the instruction programme. Remedial tutorials are organised for the benefit of those students who require revision of the instruction programme. Usually, both types of tutorial are on an individual basis. The size of groups attending module three courses varies up to a maximum of twenty. Classes are held in a flexible, well-equipped seminar room in the LRC complex. The staff manual for the LRC lays down, in considerable detail, the modus operandi of the information officers, eg:

'Curriculum design—each course must be designed through the systems approach. Aims and objectives should be set for each syllabus. Teaching schedule, teaching method, course work, reading lists, etc, should be set out according to the method adopted for Polytechnic courses.

Teaching method—the most suitable teaching methods to achieve the objectives should be employed; methods will include live lectures, seminars, tutorials, informal discussions and a variety of audio-visual learning packages. In order that students should receive the same level and content of instruction, all classes should be taught according to the common scheme of work to be followed by all information officers.

Arranging classes—the teaching programme should be made known to members of staff, usually by means of personal contact. Classes are arranged after discussion with the course tutor who should be encouraged to participate especially in module three.

Sunderland Polytechnic

At Sunderland Polytechnic instruction to all readers, including staff, postgraduates, and students, forms part of the job specification of each faculty librarian. A high reader to subject librarian ratio means that few personalised services can be provided and so the emphasis is on promoting reader self-sufficiency. An example of the type of instructional course used to achieve this is provided for the science faculty students. The course is at four broad levels:

a) Basic introduction to the service—one hour introduction for new students. Outline: Library location and arrangement; classification; location of books using catalogues and the subject index; procedures for borrowing, reservations and interlibrary loans; photocopying; special collections; short loan collection; where to find help. (Level one.) A guide to the polytechnic library service is freely available.

b) Introduction to subject literature—Suitable for second and third year students. Outline: In relation to the relevant subject area the books, periodicals, handbooks and databooks, indexing and abstracting services, review literature; the scientific paper—its role, constitution and use; information retrieval; local library resources. (Level two.)

c) Use of specialised bibliographical tools—Suitable for 3rd year students, postgraduates and staff. Outline: In relation to the relevant subject area the use of indexing, abstracting and current awareness services; information retrieval from periodicals, review literature, databooks and handbooks eg *Beilstein*, patents and standards; computerised information retrieval; translations; introduction to essay and project work. (Level three.)

d) Postgraduate instruction—Outline: Exhaustive literature searching, current awareness; information retrieval; thesis presentation; citation behaviour; computerised information retrieval. (Level four.)

Instructional courses of this type began at the prompting of the library in the early 1970s. This initiative showed there to be a latent demand for such courses. The approach made to each department to establish a suitable course depends very much on the structure of that department. Sometimes approaches are made directly to the head of department, sometimes to course leaders, by letter to all faculty members, or via the postgraduates. The library is represented by the faculty librarians on the boards of study and so is involved at the developmental stages of new courses. This has proved to be an advantage in the establishment of bibliographical instruction courses. Timing of courses is such that they coincide with the commencement of projects. In the science faculty all students receive a level three course. This usually takes one hour although some groups of students receive three hours instruction. The students are taught in groups of six to ten. No practical work is involved, one reason being that the lectures are given in the departments, not in the library. No formal feedback channels exist though contact is made with the course tutor after the completion of the projects to assess qualitatively the effects of the instruction on the performance of the students.

In addition to providing bibliographic instruction, some faculty librarians at Sunderland are also involved in general studies teaching.

110

The course is usually based around the theme of communications and includes relevant aspects of library instruction and the broader aspects of contemporary information problems. A team teaching approach makes use of the special interests of the staff, eg computers, industrial information. The library is also being encouraged to assist in the teaching of a DipHE course in communication of science information.

Trent Polytechnic

Trent Polytechnic began its library instruction programme in 1972 because it felt that students had no knowledge of what the library could offer. Heads of departments were approached in an attempt to formalise an orientation programme in the first term. This succeeded to the extent that that programme now covers 95% of new students. Instructional courses were offered to course tutors in every department. Only a minority, mainly in science, responded. Courses are run by the library subject specialists just before the students start project work, in either the second or third year. A four-hour package, lasting either a whole morning or a whole afternoon, is presented. A fifteen minute introductory tape/slide on sources of information is shown first. This is followed by a practical session of forty-five minutes on quick reference material which takes place in the seminar room. A twenty-five minute tape/slide presentation showing a simulated literature search follows. A brief literature search exercise is then undertaken for one hour before the group reassembles for the final hour to discuss the problems that are likely to emerge in the students' individual projects. A package of handouts, which includes notes on literature searching techniques, how to organise references, sources of information etc, is distributed.

Supervision of the practical work means that the group size for each course is limited to six which makes the course very labour intensive. In order to make the package a coherent whole, tape/slides have been produced for each course. It was felt that the inclusion of elements of the SCONUL cooperative tape/slide programme would make the packages disjointed. Although it is suggested that the package concept be adopted, this approach is not favoured by all the subject librarians at Trent Polytechnic. Some believe that the individual teacher should be able to adopt the approach best suited to his own temperament.

Hull University

Hull University provides a bibliographical instruction programme for postgraduate research students from all thirty-five departments but does not offer courses to undergraduates on a formal basis. All senior library staff (including the librarian) are involved because, although the library is organised on a functional basis, all assistant librarians are involved in a subject liaison scheme. The courses last one day and are held in the library. On assembly each student is given a bibliography of his subject and is then guided round the library using the bibliography as the basis for the tour. After coffee the students are given a set of questions which they have until mid-afternoon to answer. Discussion of the problems raised follows the tea break.

Each student gets an individual letter, produced by tape typewriter, inviting him to attend. In addition, supervisors and heads of departments are contacted to ask them to persuade their research students to come along. The students are asked to inform the library of their research topic so that examples and questions can be devised which bear some relation to that topic, though only one set of questions is produced for each subject group. The time involved in the preparation for this programme is considerable and is difficult to fit in with functional work. This is one reason why undergraduate courses are not given on a formal basis. Departments are beginning to ask the library to provide courses for undergraduates largely because of the increasing use of project work in undergraduate courses. Half day courses are given but no practical work is involved. Very often these courses are timetabled to occur after examinations in the summer term of the second year to help students in anticipation of their third year requirements. As the demand at this time grows, a conflict is developing with the regular library stock-taking programme which occupies the time of the staff at this particular period.

Bristol University

An interesting development at Bristol University is the instruction given to second year students in the physics department. At the end of the summer term the students are able to opt for a period of two weeks for one of a number of courses on techniques. Library instruction is one of these techniques and is thus in competition for the students' consideration with glass-blowing, etc. A normal sized group opting for library instruction is around seven. These students become almost part of the Maria Mercer Physics Library (a departmental library) for the period of two weeks. The objectives of the course are to illustrate techniques of information retrieval in physics and related subjects; to enable the student to use the various bibliographical tools in the library; and to assist the student in his own organisation and retrieval of information.

The course begins with a literature search aiming to find several general accounts or reviews on a not-too-specialised subject. Three days are allowed for the completion of this short bibliography. Problems encountered with various forms of literature during this period, eg books, journals, reviews, conferences etc, are the subject of discussions which the librarian holds with the group. At the end of this period, the students are able to embark on a second type of literature search—one where all possible information on a very specific subject is required

112

From day five until the end of the course is spent on compiling this bibliography. At the same time, informal discussions are held to examine other forms of literature and the different techniques and difficulties involved. Outside sources and services are also considered. Days eight and nine are concerned with techniques relevant to third year project work, eg report writing, personal indexes, etc. Day ten is given over to discussion of the completed bibliographies and of the course itself.

The course is 80% practical and 20% theory. Each morning there is an hour-long seminar on sources or techniques. The remainder of the day is given over to an assignment or a question sheet. Each of these (apart from the two bibliographies) is a one day exercise. Thus the student learns by self-instruction but with library staff on hand if help is required. Several handouts on sources of information in physics are also available to aid the student. The bibliographies which the students undertake during the fortnight are ones that have been commissioned by members of staff and the students are encouraged to contact them while working on the project.

Loughborough University

One of the few university libraries to cover all courses with its instructional programmes is Loughborough. Library courses began about ten years ago and have steadily built up over the years to the complete coverage of today. The first full time appointment in library instruction was made in 1969. Here, as in many of the technological universities and some newer universities, the functional roles of teaching and provision of information services are combined. This has proved useful as a number of literature search queries have been picked up during discussions with personal contacts. The provision of acceptable answers to these queries has gone a long way to creating an atmosphere of confidence in which the academic staff find it acceptable to encourage their students to attend courses organised by the library. There was some initial resistance from some of the academic staff who felt that the library teachers lacked the necessary subject knowledge. However this has been overcome by the quality of the instruction provided.

One member of the library staff, who does not teach on any of the courses, is responsible for the organisation of the courses, arranging convenient dates with departments and suitable times, ensuring a room is available and preparing the question sheets to be used in the practical sessions. Wherever possible the course is included in the student's timetable, perhaps in conjunction with similar topics, eg communications. What the student needs to know from the course is determined by reading the literature on the information requirements of particular disciplines and by discussing with individual departments what is expected of their students.

113

Students attending all undergraduate and postgraduate courses receive bibliographic instruction. The thirty-two undergraduate groups are all first year groups except for fourth year mechanical and chemical engineers. There are eleven postgraduate courses, plus one group which only visits the library for an extended tour. Instruction is given to undergraduates during their first year as this is the stage when the academic departments find it easier to make time for the course. During their first year undergraduates take other courses, eg report writing, ethics of the profession, how to study, which can easily be combined with bibliographic instruction for timetabling purposes. Ideally the library would prefer to see the students immediately prior to their long projects and dissertations, but since most students also have to do a project in their first year, this timing is not as adverse as it appears at first sight.

The programme for undergraduate courses normally takes the form of three separate one hour talks on information retrieval given in the department, a one hour visit to the library and three hours practical work (in the student's own time). The talks are often timetabled for the same time each week, but practice varies according to the department. In addition, should the department require it, three hours are spent on communication. Postgraduate groups also receive three hours on information retrieval plus two hours supervised practical work. If the course forms part of the departmental assessment (either in the form of an examination question or assessed course work) attendance is of the order of 90 to 100%. Attendance at other courses varies depending on the amount of publicity and encouragement given by the department. It averages 60 to 70%.

The first lecture deals with general background, sources of information, recorded information (literature) and finding tools, and includes a briefing for the first practical session. Lecture two covers basic information retrieval techniques in preparation for the second practical session (the tape/slide *Introduction to information retrieval* produced locally is often used), and the final lecture covers other information retrieval techniques, current awareness and the future. Personal indexes and computerised information services may be mentioned but not report writing, which forms part of the communication course. The lecture approach is used and the minimum number of handouts, except for the question sheets, are used. A different question sheet is prepared for each student. This causes considerable problems in the generation of sufficient combinations of standard questions by rotation so that students cannot collaborate.

Questions sheet one covers the tracing of an introductory text on some defined aspect of the subject, bibliographical details of a book of given title, a physical or chemical constant or element of data, the

114

tracing of an industrial organisation specialising in a particular field, and one other reference question angled towards the subject discipline. The second question sheet requires details of two recent articles in a specified subject area, the name and address of a manufacturer of a certain material, the number and date of a British Standard on a specified subject, plus one other question of general interest usually of a statistical nature. The marked questionnaires are given back to the students by the course tutors. The library corrects any mistakes of a bibliographical nature, but encourages the student to seek help from the course tutor if the mistake is due to a misunderstanding of the subject content. The postgraduate questions are more difficult, and the students often substitute their own topic within the framework of questions.

Very little evaluation of the courses is undertaken. A questionnaire was used in 1971. It employed a five point scale but the mixed nature of the replies gave no indication of the way in which to proceed. Informal feedback is obtained from course tutors.

Durham University

At Durham University there are no subject specialists as such, though most of the assistant librarians have subject responsibilities towards particular departments as well as their functional duties. This responsibility includes instructing readers in how to use the library and its resources to best advantage in their particular fields. Most librarians give at least one period of instruction to first year students, but in only a few cases has it been possible to arrange for more than one period or, indeed, to follow up this instruction in the second or third years.

New undergraduates in history and politics are shown the general library tape/slide and are given a conducted tour. The assistant librarian covering this area relies on personal contacts with members of staff to provide follow-up for the history students. Moreover, she is in the fortunate position of being on the Board of Studies in Politics and on the Staff-Student Committee. Feedback from, and knowledge of the needs of politics students are, therefore, obtained in good time. As the students approach their dissertations they are seen individually by the assistant librarian before they settle on a project title. In this way the resources required for the topic can be examined and if it is likely that, for example, too little of the necessary material is available locally, the slant of a project can be altered. After the titles have been agreed by the departments, the students are again seen individually to discuss in more detail both their topics and the sources of help available. Individual tutorials provide the most immediate feedback. The same help is provided for postgraduate research students. The problem with tuition on this individual level is one of timetabling as nearly all of the students need help at the same time. This means that up to twenty history

115

undergraduates require help in the summer term, following the twelve to fifteen politics students needing help in the spring term. One of the reasons for the adoption of this pattern is that the assistant librarian feels that, for the diverse topics covered and sources required, there is no other way to teach the history students. It might, however, be possible to treat the politics students as a group. She places a very high priority on instruction as a part of her role as a liaison officer and feels that the teaching ought to be developed further. However the demand for this must come from the departments.

Bradford University

Bradford University provides a final example of instruction in practice. In 1959 only one library instructional course, for postgraduate polymer scientists, was being given. The library began 'missionary work' and by 1965 twelve schools of study were covered and in 1971 library instruction was written into the university regulations.

Teaching is by subject specialists in various areas, of which engineering is considered here. Courses are tailored to the requirements and needs of the group. Hence some courses are given in the first year as well as in the third or fourth years depending on the timing of project work. In the first year, one or two hours are spent on sources of information. However, chemical engineers, who are required to make wide use of the library in respect of the three or four long essays associated with the courses in communication and the engineer in society, receive four hours given over to a case study. A final year course occupies four to eight hours and is given as two half days, one whole day or spread over several weeks, depending on course needs. Lectures are given to groups of forty to fifty on the structure of the literature and information sources, periodical literature and abstracts and indexes, alerting services (including computerised services), search techniques illustrated by a case study tape/slide presentation, and bibliographical citation references and personal indexes. Questions or a mini-literature-search form a practical work component of one to 1½ hours. This practical work is additional to the student's own project and is designed to assess whether the student can put into practice what he has been taught. It may be too late to find this out when he is doing his own project.

One or two formal courses are held for postgraduate students but this instruction is not on such a systematic basis as for undergraduates. Staff sit in on undergraduate courses and occasional courses are conducted especially for staff. Topics included are mechanised retrieval techniques, practical library work, reference sources (in subject groups), literature search techniques, reference and citation practice, and a forum for questions and discussion. Bradford University is one of few institutions which attempts to assess the impact of its courses.

116

Problems and limitations

Though much effort has gone into developing user education over the last few years there are, nevertheless, significant problems still to be faced.

Many librarians hold the view that the main limitation to the progress of user education is the attitude of academic staff and the teaching techniques they adopt. Although they agree in principle that students should learn to use the library and the literature of their subjects, staff do not put much emphasis on this by making it necessary for students to use the library to succeed with their courses. Students naturally consider that their main objective is to pass the exams, and if they can do so without learning efficient literature searching techniques they feel that learning such techniques does not have a high priority.

It is not just academic staff who give user education a low priority. Librarians also often rate user education low in the list of library functions. For example, one librarian believes that 'user education is an essential function of the library but its value is often exaggerated and its effects are unlikely to be experienced by more than a small minority of readers. I would not give it priority over the basic library services; the acquisition of books and periodicals, the provision of catalogues and classification, and so on.' Such a view of the place of user education in the library's priorities is widely held. Libraries which show the greatest commitment to user education are, in general, in the polytechnics and the technological universities.

Librarians in the smaller institutions find it easier to provide ad hoc individual advice and help to users, and faculty libraries tend to have closer and more informal day-to-day relations with users. These libraries are smaller and therefore less intimidating to the user and it is easier to discover the resources of the library by browsing. This, however, can cause problems in institutions where the faculty or departmental libraries are not part of the main library. In such cases it is often much more difficult to introduce user education courses into those departments enjoying the facilities of their own small library and personal help. Parochialism is very hard to overcome.

Many librarians involved in teaching programmes admit that their other library duties leave them little time to prepare and develop syllabuses, lectures, and teaching aids. Despite this, there is very little cooperative effort in the user education field even where there are several institutions of higher education in close proximity. Some libraries express concern about duplication of effort, especially in the production of teaching aids. Others, however, think that cooperation and the production of material and courses relevant to the local situation are irreconcilable.

One final problem is best expressed by Surrey University. 'Overall, it seems that most students who attend library courses find them worthwhile. The most pressing problem is to encourage those who do not attend, to do so.'

The future

It is easy to lose sight of an ideal when working in a non-ideal world. Librarians engaged in user education have little time to speculate about ideal solutions to the problems that exist and even less time to experiment and to effect changes. Many librarians see the future in terms of simplification of libraries, particularly in terms of better guiding of buildings, not just in the directional sense but also in the provision of information.

The encouragement of non-users and non-attenders of courses was mentioned by many in the survey. Attitudes to libraries ought to be shaped much earlier in a student's career and the knowledge of how to use them communicated. The ideal seen by many is a user education programme beginning in school and continuing through higher education. Although some excellent programmes in schools are already in operation, notably in the Sheffield City Libraries School Instruction Service, much more could be done at this level which would benefit students and prepare them for similar programmes in higher education.

Closer cooperation with academic staff is seen by many as the key to solving the problem of motivation of students and of providing a greater relevance to user education. In this respect integration—a common word in educational circles—has taken on a new meaning, but a meaning that is different for different people:

a) User education is more valuable if it can be integrated into the pattern of the course. In this case the student gets information and learns techniques just as he knows that they are useful, and can have a genuine reason for practising what he has learned. This means a closeness to course tutors and an expenditure of time in planning which we have not yet achieved.

b) Courses should be timetabled into the student's curriculum so that time is not wasted each year in organising the seminars. They should be programmed throughout the student's course developing over the years from an elementary class to a detailed bibliographic session scheduled at appropriate times in their course.

The ideal solution to problems of integration envisaged by City University is 'the formulation of overall objectives for courses in departments, incorporating the objectives of library instruction, and the cooperative development of instructional methods between the library and the department to see that these objectives are attained. This cannot be done until the majority of departmental staff are convinced of the benefits of effective library use, and it is, therefore, important at this stage to continue to provide a good service to them when they ask for it and to keep them actively informed of the facilities and resources available.' This sums up the view of those seeking the advancement of user education. It is a process that carries a little further the developments already begun in polytechnics in course proposals for CNAA degrees, and is not dissimilar to the library college concept often propounded in the American professional literature.

Fortunately the future is likely to be characterised by more research into the problems of user education than has hitherto been the case. This results from the activities of the Review Committee on Education for Information Use, established by the British Library Research and Development Department in 1974, whose brief was to review research and related work in the field of user education, to identify gaps in past and present research in the field, to consider steps to be taken to ensure practical action and to report to BLRDD recommending objectives and a programme of further research.

Several of the recommendations of the committee have already been acted upon, notably in creating an effective focus for the coordination, interchange and dissemination of ideas and information on activities relevant to user education. This has been achieved by the appointment of an Information Officer for User Education (based at Loughborough University). In addition the BLRDD will maintain close links with the SCONUL Information Services Group whose aims include the encouragement of cooperation in the provision of information services and the promotion of dissemination of information on such services. An immediate result of these activities has been the appearance of two new journals, *Infuse* and *ISG news*, which are enabling interested parties to share experiences of user education in a way not possible before.

Research work is now in progress and supported by BLRDD includes work on user education in schools, on travelling workshops and visual exploitation of library resources. Work on user education in schools is at an early stage and Liverpool Polytechnic is involved in the establishment of a register of the methods used to instruct pupils in the effective use of information resources. The Royal College of Art is engaged on research into the ways in which information presented on book labels, in visual guides to library catalogues, on plans and directional signs etc can be presented for maximum legibility and comprehension.

The aims of the experimental travelling workshops established by Newcastle Polytechnic are to show teaching and library staff how various aspects of information handling might be taught and incorporated into the students' curricula. They are also designed to make students aware of the sources of information in their field and how to use them effectively. Originally the workshops consisted of lectures supported by slides and a handbook. This was made up of brief notes to accompany the lecture, diagrams and flow charts, sample entries from sources, and lists of sources. It was designed to aid the students during the course and as a reference source afterwards. The lectures and handbook were supplemented by practical exercises and an extensive display. Reactions from the students of early workshops consistently showed the lecture method was not favoured and that the students preferred doing practical work. In later workshops therefore the lectures were excluded or minimised, being replaced by self-access tape/slides. The workshops were far more built around practical exercises with the handbook becoming self-instructional. One interesting component of the project is the evaluation of the workshops. Illuminative evaluation is being used and the results of the application of this technique will be very valuable to the user education field in general.

CHAPTER TEN

User education in Scandinavia

DURING THE SEVENTIES there has been a growing interest in library user education in Denmark, Finland, Norway and Sweden. This can be seen in a variety of ways: by the number of surveys and discussions on user education; by the introduction of the subject of user education into the curricula of the Scandinavian library schools; by the fact that user instruction has been the theme for papers at library conferences; and, most important of all, by the growing number of courses in user education at individual libraries. This chapter will give a short description of some of the recent developments in user education in Scandinavia.

Denmark

In Denmark a number of surveys concerned with user education have been carried out. In 1970 a round-table conference was held at Aarhus University Library (Vejledning af . . . 1971). Reports on user education in some of the largest academic libraries in Denmark were presented. These included Det Konglige Bibliotek (the Royal Library), Aarhus University Library and the Library of the Danish University of Technology, Lyngby, Copenhagen. In addition there were reports from some educational departments which offered courses in library use as part of their curricula—for example the department of history at the University of Copenhagen, where a comprehensive course of some seventy-five hours is given (Kolding Nielsen). A special handbook has been prepared for this course (Jørgensen, B, et al, 1970).

Discussions at the Aarhus conference resulted in two recommendations.

1 That the Danish Library Association (Danmarks Biblioteksförening, Gruppe D) or the Joint Council of Danish Research Libraries (Forsknings-bibliotekernes Fællesråd) should organise a collection of teaching materials which would then be available for use by all academic libraries in Denmark.

2 That the same organisations should contact appropriate persons or committees at universities and other institutions of higher education in order to discuss the possibilities for integrating library instruction in the various curricula.

A comparative study of user education in Scandinavian academic libraries (Fjällbrant, 1975) showed that user education courses were given at a number of academic libraries such as the Library of the Danish University of Technology, Copenhagen, (Jørgensen, F, 1967) and the Central Library of Botany, Copenhagen (Christiansen, 1971).

The most recent survey dates from August 1976. This survey was carried out by the Library Committee of the National Research Council (Forskningsrådenes Biblioteksutvalg. *Undervisning i litteratursøgning...*) The conclusions drawn by Lau from this material, which was obtained by studying and extrapolating the official curricula and study schedules of various institutions of higher education, were that library instruction in Denmark was sporadic in the sense that whether or not any teaching takes place depends on whether there happens to be a person around who is interested in offering such courses. No staff are hired to carry out such teaching as their primary assignment. Most often this type of work has third or fourth priority for the staff of research libraries in Denmark.

Apart from being sporadic, library instruction also tends to be organised arbitrarily in the sense that in many libraries there is no permanent organisational framework for this type of activity. In some cases, the opposite problem emerges, as when a library adopts a rigid schedule for a course of this type and sticks to it year after year without adapting it to the changes in study habits and university curricula that have taken place meanwhile.

An attempt has been made to define goals and objectives for user education in 1974, by a subcommittee of the Research Libraries' Committee for Goals and Objectives (Forskningsbibliotekernes Fællesråds Målsætningsutvalg). This committee produced a report in which a model of the general principles and framework for user education was presented. It included discussions on educational principles, course structure and content. *(Undervisning i litteratursøgning, 1975).* This report has served as a starting point for discussion on user education and for the development of individual library courses.

Some aspect of user education has been presented at a number of library conferences in Denmark. In addition to the round-table conference at Aarhus mentioned above, user education was the theme of a meeting of the Danish Research Libraries at Roskilde in 1976, the subject of a paper at the XIII Nordic Library Associations Meeting at Aarhus, in 1976, and the topic for an international seminar—'Users and librarians' held at Roskilde in November 1976. At this seminar an attempt was made to discuss the needs and form for library user education with students, academic staff and librarians. Student expectations were compared with the actual situation met when trying to obtain information in connection with their studies.

At the Royal Library School in Copenhagen, various aspects of user education—goals and objectives, teaching methods, etc—have been included in the advanced courses for librarians since 1974, and in 1976/77 two courses on libraries, their use, and user education, were given for university teachers. These latter courses proved so successful that further courses of a similar kind are planned.

Many of the university libraries now organise some form of user education. The Library of the Danish University of Technology, at Copenhagen, has been particularly active in promoting user education for engineering students and for engineers. During the academic year 1976/77, there has been a reorganisation of this user education programme—courses are now available for *all* engineering departments. The courses are arranged in modules, so that students can select and combine different units to suit their own particular needs (Jørgensen, 1977).

Two new university centres have been opened in Denmark during the seventies—Roskilde University Centre in 1972 and Aalborg University Centre in 1973. At these new institutions the teaching is strongly project-based, and this has enabled the development of library instruction which is directly linked to the project work carried out by the students, as described in chapter eight. This type of instruction has considerable relevance to student needs and this results in a high degree of student motivation towards the instruction given. At Roskilde members of staff from the Department of Education have worked together with library staff, to develop methods of instruction suitable for the project type of learning and in the evaluation of these methods, in practical teaching situations.

Research on user education is being carried out, in Denmark, by both individual research workers and by a number of institutions, amongst which is the Royal Library School at Copenhagen, where a central index of research projects within this field is being compiled. Research is being carried out for example in the following areas—literature searching in psychological education, (Clod-Poulsen, 1975), on the user-librarian negotiation process (Timmermann and Ingwersen, Johansen and Timmermann), and on literature searches and the use of literature in connection with project-organised studies (Berman et al).

Finland

In 1967, TINFO—the Finnish Council for Scientific and Technical Information—appointed a committee to study the organisation of user instruction for the effective use of information sources and services. This committee, amongst other things, sent out in 1969 a questionnaire on user instruction to twenty-four academic libraries. They found that of these four had courses of between six and twenty hours on the use of information sources, whilst seven libraries held shorter courses at irregular intervals. (Kommittébetänkande, 1970).

The committee put forward the recommendations that all students should receive training in the use of information sources and that this instruction should take place in the academic libraries, under the guidance of librarians/information officers. Instruction should include 'the use of the university library' and 'use of information sources and information services'. Students, research workers and academic staff should be taught the use of computer-based information retrieval. The committee recommended the provision of special funds for these purposes, but in actual practice user instruction within the academic libraries in Finland has been financed by funds from their respective universities.

These recommendations acted as a stimulus for the development of user education within the academic libraries. In 1974, nineteen of twenty-four research libraries had some form of library orientation, fourteen gave courses at undergraduate level, two at postgraduate level and six gave courses for 'other' groups—industrial engineers, nurses, etc.

The position in 1977 has been summed up by Uuttu: 'Instruction in the use of libraries and in information retrieval is making rapid progress in research libraries in Finland'. All but one of the university libraries offers a short library orientation course. Instruction in the use of information media and information services is a regular part of the teaching programme at the universities of Turku, Oulu, Jyväskylä, Kuopio, and Joensuu, as well as within some departments at the University of Helsinki. Courses of user instruction are also given at Tampere and Helsinki Universities of Technology. These courses, which always include practical work, vary in length between ten and twenty hours. The teaching is carried out by information specialists from the library working in co-operation with university academic staff. In some universities the instruction is compulsory, in others optional.

During recent years, a number of libraries have produced audio-visual programmes on the use of the library and/or information retrieval. This is in contrast to the situation in 1974, when few libraries made use of this type of material. One example of the experimental production and use of audio-visual videotape material is to be seen at the Central Medical Library, Helsinki, where programmes on MEDLINE computer-based information retrieval and an orientation on the use of the library have been made (Öberg). Videotape programmes have also been produced and used in courses for engineering students at the Helsinki University of Technology Library (Kivelä).

At the Helsinki University of Technology Library—the national central library for technology in Finland—considerable attention has been paid to the question of reader education in the use of the library and its collections. User studies carried out by Erkko in 1970 and Törnudd in 1973, revealed the need for user education. The university library organised a programme of instruction which consists of compulsory courses for first year students—about 800 per year. It is intended to carry out evaluation on these freshmen courses in the near future. In addition, optional subject-orientated courses in information retrieval are given in a number of areas of technology. At present these optional courses are attended by 15% to 20% of the undergraduates. Video programmes and tape/slides are used as teaching aids, and these are supplemented by guides to the use of the library and a number of subject bibliographies.

Norway

One of the first Scandinavian seminars on 'Library user instruction' (sponsored by NORDDOK) was held in Oslo in early 1974. In Norway the subject of user education was introduced into the curriculum of the College of Librarianship in the academic year 1973/74. Pioneering work on the use of audio-visual material for library instruction has been carried out at NSI (Norsk Senter for Informatikk) where a tape/slide introduction was produced for use with a special compendium on information retrieval. This has been used in technical colleges and at industrial firms.

In 1974, whilst many of the libraries had some courses for students, they had far fewer courses than they would have liked to have had. However, during the years 1974 to 1977, new courses in library instruction have been introduced and developed at many Norwegian university libraries.

At the main university library of Oslo the library staff arrange guided tours and give library instruction at various levels, in response to requests. Most of the library instruction is, however, at the faculty libraries. Thus special courses have been developed at the library of the Faculty of Social Sciences, for both new students and advanced students requiring material for an undergraduate thesis (Kvam). During the academic year 1976/77, at the Faculty of Humanities Library, a librarian was appointed with the responsibility to develop a programme of user instruction. This programme consists of an initial orientation, followed by a second period of instruction during the first term, and subsequent instruction at later points of study (Haaland).

At the University of Bergen, an automated tape/slide programme has been produced and this is used as an orientation for new students. For advanced students instruction on bibliographies and information retrieval is given, on request, by the staff of the faculty libraries.

At the University of Trondheim there is a well-developed programme of user education at the University of Technology library (Gjersvik). Courses are held at different levels. Regular introductory lectures are given for about 600 new students every year, and three to ten hour courses are offered for advanced students. In addition special courses are held on specific topics such as 'The use of *Science citation index*' and 'Computer-based information retrieval' and 'The use of patents'. Courses are given for external users such as industrial engineers, and for other institutions of higher education.

In the other faculties at the University of Trondheim—science, medicine, social sciences and arts—library user education has been introduced during the last few years, but varies considerably according to subject. In the science faculty, regular instruction is provided at introductory and more advanced levels and printed guides on the use of the library and bibliographical aids have been produced. In the arts and social sciences faculties instruction is less regular—all new students are offered elementary library instruction, but at later stages the courses vary widely in regularity, length and content, according to the subject. Haaland stated, in 1977, that 'it is very noticeable in all subjects that the average new user lacks basic library skills.'

The University of Tromsø, which was founded in 1972, is the youngest Norwegian university. User education was introduced by the library in the academic year 1976/77. A three stage programme has been planned: a one-hour orientation for new students, a two-hour introduction to literature searching for undergraduates and a longer course with practical exercises for postgraduates. Use is being made of SCONUL tape/slide material from England.

Sweden

In 1973 many of the academic libraries had some form of optional library orientation or instruction, but many of these courses were short guided tours. Little evaluation of user education courses had been carried out.

During the years 1974 to 1977 there has been a marked interest in library user education in Sweden. This can be seen in a number of ways: by the introduction of the subject 'user education' into the curriculum of the final term of studies at the College of Librarianship, Borås, from 1974 onwards; by the provision of a grant by the Office of the Chancellor of the Swedish Universities, in June 1975, for an education project involving several university libraries; by the fact that papers on some aspect of user education were presented at a number of Swedish library conferences, and that this subject was the topic for a Swedish round-table conference in November 1975, followed by an Anglo-Scandianvian seminar on the same theme in November 1976 (sponsored by the Scandinavian Research Librarians Association), and most important of all by the growing number of courses in library user education at various Swedish academic libraries. This growth in library user education was clearly shown in a study of the development of user education programmes in Swedish academic libraries in the years 1973-1977 (Fjällbrant, 1977). The number of libraries offering some form of user instruction had increased during this period, but the most remarkable change was in the increase in the variety and length of the courses offered at individual university libraries.

The most comprehensive programme of user education was to be seen at Chalmers University of Technology Library, Gothenburg, where a systematic programme had been developed during the years 1973 to 1977 (see chapter seven). This programme consisted of four parts: library orientation for approximately 900 new users per year; a fourteen-hour introductory course in information retrieval for about 800 engineering undergraduates per year; thirty-five-hour courses in information retrieval for postgraduates; and seminars on information retrieval for industrial engineers.

The libraries at other universities of technology have also been active in the promotion of user education. Thus the library of the Royal Institute of Technology, Stockholm, has organised many seminars on information retrieval for research workers and engineers (Gluchowicz). A new type of course for engineering students was introduced in autumn 1976 (Sabsay), consisting of introductory lectures followed by practical sessions in manual and computer-based information retrieval.

At Luleå University of Technology, founded in 1971, a comprehensive programme of user education has been developed during the seventies (Marklund). Every year, some 300 new students take part in a two-hour library orientation in connection with a general university course on 'Technology in society'. Twelve to sixteen hour courses on information retrieval are provided for undergraduate engineering students and an advanced course of forty hours is planned for postgraduates.

At the engineering faculty at Linköping University, founded in 1970, another three level programme of user education has been devised, with one to two hour courses in library orientation and courses in information retrieval for undergraduates and postgraduates (Lindberg). These courses form part of a programme which includes students from the arts and medical faculties. An introductory tape/slide guide—*The university library and its services* has been produced during 1976, together with a general guide to information retrieval and a number of subject bibliographies.

User education has also been promoted at other university libraries serving the needs of specialised user groups, such as medical students—

127

at the biomedical section of Gothenburg University Library (Fjällbrant, 1976), at the Karolinska Institute Library, Stockholm (Ljungars), and agricultural students—at the Swedish University of Agriculture Library, Ultuna (Fjällbrant and Westberg, 1974).

The libraries at other new universities such as Umeå, founded in 1963, Örebro, founded in 1976 as a branch of Uppsala University, and Växjö, founded in 1967 as a branch of Lund University, have also shown considerable interest in the subject of library user education.

At Stockholm University, an established multi-faculty university with a large number of students, the opening of the new university library building in 1971, signalled the start of considerable development work in user education. Now, in 1977, an introductory guided tour is provided for about 500 new students every year, and a short one to two hour introductory course in using the library and methods of information retrieval is given to approximately 1000 students per year. An interesting evaluation is being carried out on the comparison of user education courses arranged by the library and user education organised by individual academic departments.

Discussion

It has been shown that there is a growing interest and increased activity in library user education in the Scandinavian countries. The libraries that appear to be particularly active in this field are those serving specialised user groups—such as engineering students, medical students, agricultural students, etc, and the libraries at the most recently established universities. This would seem to correspond to the library user education situation in Britain, where the greatest impact seems to be made with scientists and engineers and at polytechnics, and at the ex-CAT and technological universities.

Reasons for interest in user education could be linked either to the nature of the subject or to the type of institution in which the teaching takes place. Estimates have been made of the growth of information and published literature within the various disciplines, and it can be seen that the rate of growth of primary literature is considerably more rapid in science and technology than in the liberal arts. This rapid growth in primary literature has resulted in a corresponding growth in secondary publications, such as abstracts and indexes, and in computerised information retrieval services. This, in turn, brings about an increased need for science and technology students to learn how to obtain the information that they require from these primary and secondary sources. Thus it could be that the development of library user education was a direct function of the rate of growth of literature. If this were so, one would expect to find that there were a greater number of courses offered to students from the faculties of natural sciences, medicine and engineering at multi-faculty universities, than to students from the arts faculty. In Sweden in 1974, Fjällbrant could find no evidence that proportionately more courses were being offered to medical, science and engineering students than to students from other faculties. In this present account there is again no evidence to support the theory that the growth of user education is dependent on the growth of information within a field of studies.

This would suggest that the development of library user education is partly dependent on the type of institution of higher education. The specialised university libraries in Scandinavia serve student populations of limited size (up to about 6000 students) and their students have rather similar curricula. The new universities, while serving students from several faculties, have often smaller student populations than the older established universities. Moreover in many of the older universities individual teaching departments are often spread over a large geographical area.

In this connection, it is particularly interesting to study the development of user education at Stockholm University Library. The new library was opened in 1971 and serves a multi-faculty student population of 27000 students. Against this background the library has started a comprehensive programme of user education, with library orientation for over 500 students per year and short introductory courses in information retrieval for over 1000 students per year. At the University of Oslo most of the library instruction is given at the faculties on the university campus at Blindern. This campus, originally established in the thirties, expanded considerably during the sixties. At Lund, in Sweden, the new university library is approaching completion. This library will serve students from the medical, science and engineering faculties. During the planning and design of this library, attention has been paid to the creation of a positive user situation, with clear layout and good sign-posting. There are also plans to develop a programme of user education in connection with the opening of the library. Thus it would seem that the building of a new university library or campus appears to act in some cases as a stimulus for the initiation and active development of library user education.

Conclusion

There has been a growing interest in library user education in the Scandianvian countries during the seventies. This has resulted in an increasing number of courses of orientation and instruction at many academic libraries.

There is a need for continuing interest in this aspect of librarianship, which can contribute to improving the efficiency of the libraries by leading to increased use of the resources that they contain. At the recent Anglo-Scandinavian Seminar on User Education, held at Gothenburg in November 1976, recommendations were put forward about the need and form for future Scandianvian cooperation in this area. It was suggested that a central reference collection of library user education material should be set up. This collection should include teaching material and papers/articles on user education. A start has been made on this work at Chalmers University of Technology Library, Gothenburg. It was also recommended that a Nordic Committee on Library User Education should be set up, and it is hoped that the Scandinavian Research Librarians' Association will take the initiative and define the scope and activities for such a committee, in the near future.

CHAPTER ELEVEN

User education in the USA

TO GIVE an overview of the present state of user education in the United States would in many senses be to repeat what has already been said in chapter nine about the United Kingdom. Given the different academic situations, the present state of the art is very similar in the two countries, though the history of user education in theory and practice is longer in the US, as evidenced, for example, by the reviews of Bonn and Givens. It is not intended to repeat what has been said elsewhere but rather to note trends and highlight differences that exist in user education in the US. This in itself must be superficial because the diversity and number of institutions is so immense that an illuminative collective experience is even more impossible in the US situation than it was in the UK.

Dyson's conclusion, comparing the British and American scene, was that the commitment to library instruction programmes is more widespread in Britain than in the US, both locally and nationally, but that university libraries in the US have been more innovative in using audio-visual hardware, programmed learning work books and the like. However since there was little coordination nationally the results have had less impact than the comparatively fewer but better coordinated (and evaluated) programmes in Britain. Even a cursory glance at the literature will reveal that there is a great deal written about the theory of user education and there are many ideas for courses and yet, as Griffin and Clarke note in their 1972 survey, it is a curious paradox that instruction in library use, which so many librarians regard as one of the highest forms of library service, remains so ill-defined and poorly organised. Traditional methods of instruction are still the most important, there being little innovation in teaching methods, though audio-visual aids are given more emphasis in the total user education programme than in the UK. A greater emphasis is placed on user education at an earlier stage in the educational curriculum even as early as kindergarten, and certainly in elementary school grades.

Other important differences include the greater use of evaluation in the US for the comparison and assessment of teaching methods (though not necessarily for measuring the achievement of individual programmes or courses) and the concentration on freshman orientation as the major component of a user education programme. There has recently been a move towards greater emphasis being given to the needs of more advanced students and graduates, and Dyson's survey confirms a rapid expansion of instructional programmes in the seventies. They are now receiving a higher priority than before and more money for their implementation.

The methods adopted for orientation programmes generally fall into one of five categories—tour, handbook, lecture, separate credit course, or individual instruction. The most popular of these appears to be the conducted tour. It is difficult to put a percentage figure on the number of institutions adopting this method because of the diversity of types of institution of higher education. Most surveys of user education use a different base for sampling, but all are agreed that the tour is widely used for orientation purposes. The 'walk-through' or conducted tour of the library building led by library staff is still, despite doubts and questioning as to its value, used by the majority. The fact that students are brought into physical contact with the library is thought to outweigh the disadvantages associated with the method. However, because of dissatisfaction new approaches to the tour are being tried.

The self-guided tour either in print form or on audio cassette is gaining in popularity. Advantages seen for this type of tour are that the student can proceed at his own convenience and pace, that the method encourages the student to browse, enables him to handle materials of special interest to him, and generally leads to a personal confrontation of the student with books, facilities and people, something which conducted tours tend to prevent. 'Armchair tours' providing an audiovisual (usually tape/slide or television) guided tour of the library are increasingly used as a substitute for the conducted tour and not, as in the UK, as a supplement to it.

This tendency to replace the personal dimension of user education by hardware can be seen in other aspects of user education in the USA, yet the person to person approach is still maintained to be the ideal. For example Millis asserts that 'the library must be staffed by humanists alert and consenting to the needs and problems of people, not just to the demands of accurate records . . . Can we not relate the library to (the user) so personally that he is able to sense in it a continuum for himself and his growth? Can we not increase his sensitivity to the lateral growth of ideas by exposing him to all kinds of resources, ridding him gradually of his dependence on and regurgitation of constricted, vertical, legalistic thinking? Can we not be alive enough ourselves to awaken in him an eagerness for intellectual freedom and independence? For joy in learning? For ecstacy in education?' She concludes that orientation which involves students in a total library experience on a one-to-one basis, rather than in an assembly line of isolated exposures, cannot be anything but a commitment to help.

Handbooks or printed library guides are very often the only other form of instruction provided in many colleges and universities. The majority are traditional in format though the use of colour, illustrations and cartoons distinguishes many of them from their transatlantic counterparts. The cartoon approach is often also translated into a light-hearted, even colloquial, style of writing to which the student can relate. Explanations of, for example, the use of the catalogue, are kept simple. Such a style and approach would not find favour with English conservative tastes. The Federal Library Committee have produced a set of guidelines for library handbooks to assist in the preparation of printed materials. Included in the guidelines is information to be used in a handbook, order of presentation, style of writing, and format and design.

A cooperative venture in the production of printed teaching aids resulted in the *Pathfinders* series of publications. Originally part of the Model Library Project of Project Intrex at MIT, these publications have been described as being like maps to the resources in a library. Their function is to get users started on their information search. They are now published commercially. This again is a difference between the US and UK. Indeed there are now many handbooks commercially available providing comprehensive introductions to libraries in general and to the materials within them. Examples are J K Gates' *Guide to the use of books and libraries*, M G Cook *The new library key*, J Lolley *Your library—what's in it for you*. Subject guides are also available, an example being J R Kennedy's *Library research guide to religion and theology* which is the first of a series of research guides.

Not only are commercially published keys being made available but there is also a trend for universities and colleges to publish details of their user education programmes and make them more widely available. For example the University of Texas at Austin has produced a 100-page book entitled *A comprehensive program of user education for the general libraries* which is a guide for the development of a coordinated programme of instruction at the university. User education committees developed the programme during 1975 and 1976 and since then task forces have begun work on pilot projects for self-instruction and instruction for graduate students as a first stage in implementing the programme. Goals established for the programme are to increase user awareness of the library as a primary source of information and as an agency to which users may turn for assistance with their information ne ?s; to acquaint users with library facilities; and to help users take maximum advantage of library resources in meeting their information needs. In formulating these goals and designing the programme surveys were undertaken of student and faculty opinion and needs.

Separate orientation lectures are the least popular form of orientation both with students and librarians but they are still very common. One improvement seen by many is the move in the timing of the lecture away from the first few days of the students' course to a clinic session just prior to the writing of a term-paper. At this time the students' motivation is higher and an introduction can be made to information retrieval. The alternative to the separate lecture is the provision of a credit course, which because of its credit nature also increases motivation. These are however not common and most are elective courses attracting only minority attendance. There are other disadvantages notably the staff time required to prepare the courses adequately and, because the course has to be of a certain length to qualify for a credit, the tendency to include too much information and turn the students into mini-librarians. In addition, because of the elective nature of the courses and the fact that they are not linked to a particular subject, the spread of the students' subject interest makes it almost impossible to teach the use of subject literature in anything other than a general fashion.

Individual instruction takes one of two general formats. Point-of-use devices are gaining in popularity as are self-instructional aids generally. They are seen as the only practical way of instructing all students at a time of poor staff-student ratios. Point-of-use devices have the built-in incentive that the student will learn when he experiences a real felt need to do so. Formats adopted include tape/slide presentations and a telephone connected to an audio commentary. However all point-of-use devices have one important drawback. They serve in a sense as second level instruction since a user receives instruction in the use of a bibliographic tool only if he knows that it exists and that it is potentially useful in solving his particular problem.

Programmed instruction is found in three formats, none of which is widely used: the book, the teaching machine, and computer-aided instruction. The advantages seen for the method are similar to those for the self-guided tour—the student is engaged actively, he can work alone and at his own pace and is provided with immediate feedback, and no teacher is required, illustrating again the removal of the personal element from instruction. In addition it makes possible the presentation of subject matter in a logical manner which has been pre-tested and validated. The method has been little used altogether, except where proponents of the technique are to be found. Notably this applies to computer aided instruction at the University of Denver where student response has been enthusiastic to the short introductions to certain elements of library use that students need to know. The purpose of the programmes is mainly orientation but instruction is offered in them. An additional advantage of the method at Denver is that the programmes are available from eight in the morning to midnight.

Computer-aided instruction is potentially one of the most important of the new aids to user education and may become more so as the need to train more and more users of on-line computer based information retrieval services becomes apparent. At the present time very little instruction is given to such users in universities and colleges. CAI in conjunction with the on-line retrieval system, according to Moghdam, is the most promising form of instruction, in that medium as well as message may be used to acquaint the novice searcher with an interactive user/system interface.

Another example of the replacement of the personal element in instruction is provided by the increasing popularity of self-instruction packages. For orientation purposes UCLA's college library provides lectures on request, tours, a self-guided audio-tour and guides to the use of specific reference tools. To meet the needs of users beyond this orientation phase the library has developed a self-paced, self-directed course providing the student with twenty assignments to complete which require him to make use of the facilities and resources of the library. A work book is used to introduce the course and describe simply the sources used in each assignment, as well as pose the questions for solution. Examples of topics for assignments are: the card catalogue-subject approach, biographies, audio-room, microform. Each student (up to 100) has a different question and answer sheet. Similar assignments are included in a course developed and taught by reference staff at the University of South Florida, Tampa. The emphasis is on the practical element but here communication between librarians and students is encouraged, as it is at Brown University which provides an example of an institution augmenting its reference service staff by using students trained in reference work. These students are used both to man the reference desk during extended hours and to provide special service to undergraduates during the normal hours. It is assumed that as students they are more approachable by their fellow students. The Council on Library Resources and the National Endowment for the Humanities are supporting a programme to train eight to twelve students per year from a range of departments. Each student, on completion of the training which includes an intensive orientation to reference sources, the writing of bibliographic guides and supervised desk duties, spends nine hours a week at the reference desk and six hours liaising between library and department. This includes speaking to classes on library use and the

compilation of introductory bibliographies in their subject special-
ities.

Instruction at sophomore, senior and graduate levels is not so well
developed as at freshman level. Subject bibliographic instruction and
searching techniques are covered but courses deal with printed information sources and not, as noted above, with mechanised services. Lectures
plus audiovisual aids are the usual teaching methods employed. Course
related library instruction is often synonymous in the USA with integration which can be at a very superficial level. The ultimate in integration is the library-college approach and other examples of integrated
instruction are afforded by two comparatively smaller colleges, Earlham
and Wabash. Support for integration is afforded by the National Science
Foundation which is providing funds for a project to help institutions
develop course-related library instruction programmes. Workshops are
held at Earlham College at which a librarian and teaching faculty member
from each of the several institutions involved explore the philosophy,
problems of implementation and their solutions, for programmes of
course-related instruction in undergraduate education.

In addition, librarians from thirteen college and university libraries
are receiving support in the 1977-78 academic year from the Council
on Library Resources' Library Service Enhancement Programme to
explore with faculty, students and administrators ways of integrating the
library more fully in the educational process on campus. Several of the
programmes involve conducting workshops or seminars for faculty or
experimenting with audiovisual techniques in library orientation. Staff-
ing for user education programmes has already been seen as a problem
faced by many. The number of staff assigned to user education
varies according to the method of organisation of user education within
the library. A survey of sixty-four Association of Research Libraries
libraries published as *SPEC flyer no 17* suggests two methods for the
administration of library instruction. The first is the maintenance of a
formalised and centralised administration of library instruction within
the library, allocating responsibility for coordination to a specific person
and/or committee. The other pattern is decentralised and responsibility
is assumed by staff on a more or less ad hoc basis. Needless to say the
survey found that user education activity was greater and more diverse
with the former pattern of organisation. Dyson found that organisation
patterns of library instruction programmes reflected the local circum-
stances and conditions but he too noted that where specific posts were
created for cooperation and liaison with faculty, a greater measure of
success was achieved.

That different methods of user education are tried out and that there
is a general dissatisfaction with the methods adopted may be sympto-
matic of the fact that few programmes have stated aims and objectives.

136

Only recently has the literature begun to focus on the goals of bibliographic instruction. A significant and important development in this area was one of the last tasks of the ACRL Bibliographic Instruction Task Force, namely the provision in two parts of a set of guidelines for bibliographic instruction in academic libraries. The first part of the document deals with what constitutes an effective bibliographic instruction programme, the second part is a model statement of objectives for an entire programme of bibliographic instruction for undergraduates. Both parts are intended to be expanded in order to amplify the guidelines.

The first part of the document is based on the premise that it is a responsibility of an academic library not only to support the teaching function but to actively participate in it in instructing the community in the effective identification and use of information resources relevant to their needs and interests. Effective instructional programmes, it is suggested, are characterised by:

A written profile of the information needs of the various groups within the academic community.

A written statement of objectives including long-range and intermediate goals. The objectives will be directed to specific needs and make provision for various methods of instruction. The statement will outline methods of measuring progress toward the attainment of the objectives.

Continued and sufficient financial support identifiable in the library's budget.

Librarians and other qualified staff of status and in sufficient numbers to be responsible for planning, implementing and evaluating the programme.

Facilities, equipment and materials for the preparation and presentation of different modes of instruction.

Participation of the academic and library communities in the formulation of objectives and the evaluation of their attainment.

The written statement of objectives, it is recognised, will be of necessity unique to each institution and the product of that institution. However part two of the document is a model statement intended for the guidance of those libraries preparing their list of objectives. The general objective of a course of bibliographic instruction is stated to be that 'the student, by the time he or she completes a programme of undergraduate studies, should be able to make efficient and effective use of the available library resources and personnel in the identification and procurement of material to meet an information need.' This general objective is then broken down into meaningful units of terminal objectives of which there are four. These are further subdivided into enabling objectives, defining the specific knowledge or skills necessary for the achievement of the terminal objectives. The enabling objectives are written, so far as is possible, as behavioural objectives which are specific and measurable. Thus terminal objective four subsection b is 'the student can make effective use of the library resources available to him; he knows how to use reference tools basic to all subject areas.' The third enabling objective related to this is 'in a specified time period, the student can list five periodical titles (and the indexes which cover them) in an unfamiliar subject field using a directory such as *Ulrich's international periodicals directory'*.

This model statement is a welcome stimulus to all libraries to formulate their own statement of objectives. Though the objectives can be criticised as being low level or entirely cognitive, some indeed as being of doubtful value, they nevertheless represent an advancement in thinking on the subject of aims and objectives which will be welcomed not only in the USA but certainly also in Britain.

One of the advantages of a statement of objectives is the help it can give in evaluation of the programme. However Hackman in her proposal for a programme of library instruction, notes that a major shortcoming of American librarianship and library literature is the failure to provide critical, retrospective evaluation. She goes on to suggest that a nationally publicised programme is often deemed, ipso facto, a 'success'. Having once achieved this national recognition few institutions consider abandoning or drastically revising their 'successful' programme.

Mention has been made several times in this chapter of organisations supporting the development of user education programmes. This activity is a feature of the US scene and in concluding this overview it is appropriate to note the range of organisations involved. One of the organisations noted above, the ACRL Bibliographic Task Force, was a consortium of libraries formed to consider the possibility of establishing a clearing house for information on constructional programmes currently in operation, to explore methods of evaluation of existing programmes and materials and to investigate the needs for research into problems connected with instruction programmes. Increasing interest in the subject of user education has in 1977 led to the Association of College and Research Libraries Board of Directors establishing a Bibliographical Instruction Section within ACRL, to replace the Bibliographical Instruction Task Force. The aims of the new section will be to develop programmes to meet the needs of the membership in exploring the scope, nature and problems of operating bibliographic instruction programmes. Policy statements on bibliographic instruction as part of academic and research library services will be developed. The section will cooperate with an informally advise Project LOEX (see below) and explore methods of evaluating existing bibliographic instruction programmes and materials as well as suggesting and promoting research. It is intended also that the section should cooperate with the American Library Association's Instruction in the Use of Libraries Committee (and any other such groups with similar interests).

The latter committee's aims are:

To review on a continuing basis activities within the ALA on instruction in the use of libraries and to coordinate them with the activities of other agencies.

To recommend activities to the appropriate units of ALA and to encourage their implementation.

To coordinate these activities within the association.

To conduct studies or promote research of more than divisional concern.

To act as a clearing house for information on significant programmes of instruction.

The use of the mass media as a means of user education is being exploited by the ALA who are producing a thirty second television 'commercial' in the form of an animated message to promote the use of all types of library. Potentially the message could reach 96% of all US households. Librarians buying the programme will also receive publicity kits advising them how to arrange for showing the message on their local television stations.

The Association of Research Libraries' Office of Management Studies operates the Systems and Procedures Exchange Centre (SPEC) which collects data and documentation related to academic and research library management and is a mechanism for sharing management techniques expertise. It has produced a survey of library instruction from the management angle, *SPEC flyer no 17* which was mentioned above.

The Council on Library Resources is a private, non-profit-making organisation receiving financial support from the Ford Foundation and seeking to aid the solution of library problems, particularly academic and research libraries. It establishes and directs programmes giving grants to organisations and libraries on a contract basis. In particular twenty-four libraries in colleges and universities are on five-year plans to enhance the library's role in the education of undergraduates and to broaden the library's role on the campus.

Despite the need for coordination of all the existing activity, both nationally and locally, of organisations with very similar aims, there was established at the ALA's 1977 summer conference yet another group —a Library Instruction Round Table. The aims of this group are to provide a forum for discussion of activities, programmes and problems in the use of libraries; to contribute to the education and training of librarians for library instruction; to promote instruction in the use of libraries as an essential library service; and to serve as a channel of communication on instruction in the use of libraries.

One of the common objectives of these groups is the establishment of a freer flow of information on library instruction. This has been helped considerably by the establishment in 1972 at Eastern Michigan University of Project LOEX (Library Orientation and Instruction Exchange). This is a clearing house for both materials and information relating to academic library orientation and instruction. Its aims are to facilitate communication among libraries with instructional programmes; to assist libraries interested in developing such programmes; and to aid librarians and library science educators and students in their research endeavours. To this end it operates for its members a deposit and loan system for material and organises a travelling exhibit for conferences and meetings. An information service is provided and enquirers are put in touch with librarians likely to be able to assist them. It should be remembered though that Project LOEX is a clearinghouse and information exchange centre and is not involved in coordination of the production of instructional materials. This is an area in which considerable duplication occurs and where there is lacking in the USA anything comparable to the SCONUL cooperative tape/slide scheme.

CHAPTER TWELVE

User education and its integration into the functioning of the academic library

THE EXAMPLES given in chapter one of published material on library user education provide evidence of the growth in importance of this aspect of librarianship. The need for increased library user instruction may be partly related to the rapid growth of published material—particularly marked in certain disciplines such as science and technology. More and more people, in an ever-increasing number of countries, are engaged in scientific and technological work, and this has led to a direct rise in the publication of information. It has become increasingly difficult, because of this information explosion, for the individual student to obtain relevant information on particular topics of interest to him.

An increase in the number of academic library user education programmes may also be linked to the increase in the numbers of students taking part in higher education (and the relative decrease in the ratio of librarian to students) and to the changing form of higher education, which is moving in the direction of project-orientated studies at many institutions.

The relationship of user education to other functions of the academic library

In view of this increase in interest in library user education it is of importance to consider its role in the academic library and its relationship to the other functions of the library. User instruction is often regarded by librarians as an independent (and luxury?) function of the academic library, a function to be conveniently reduced in times of economic need. User education and computer-based methods of information retrieval are new aspects in the working of the academic library when compared with the traditional functions of acquisition, cataloguing and classification, information services and inter-library lending systems. What is the relationship between the new and the old functions?

Acquisition, cataloguing and classification can be regarded as comprising the 'input' into the library system (see figure ten). This is followed by some form of storage in closed or open-access form. The 'output' of the library is then made up of the lending activities, information retrieval

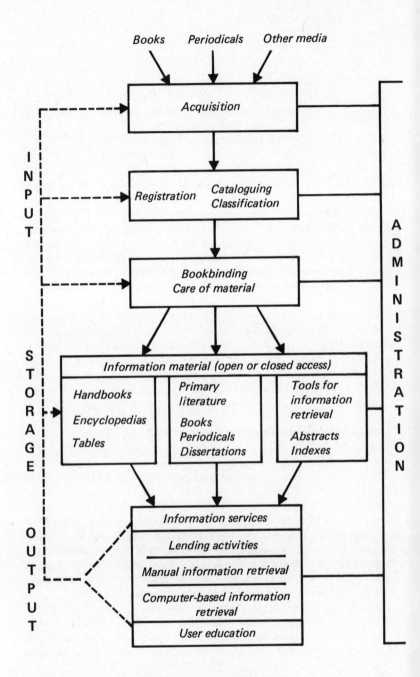

Figure 10: The library system

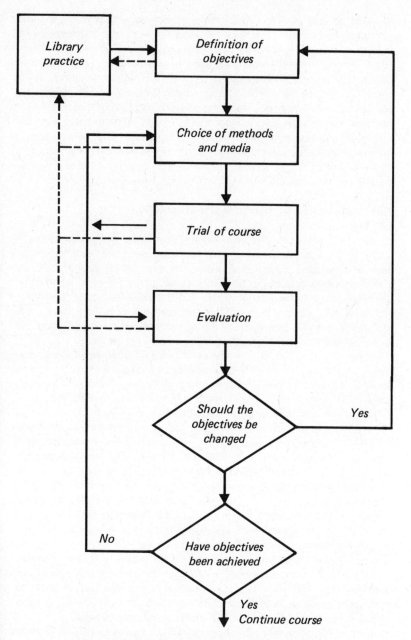

Figure 11: Development of a course of education
in relation to existing library practice

and user education. User education is concerned with enabling the user to obtain the output material he requires from the existing library system and network of connected library systems. Thus user education is an integral part of the functioning of the library. Programmes of instruction are closely dependent on the other academic library functions, such as cataloguing practice and method of storage. The objectives for courses of library user education arise, in part, out of existing library practice, and, in turn, the development of a programme of user education can exert considerable influence on this practice (see figure eleven).

Examples of the effects of user education on existing library practice in an academic library were seen in the development of the programme of user education at Chalmers University of Technology Library.

Effects of planning a programme of user education on library practice

At an early stage in the planning and development of the programme it was found that there was an interaction between the planned instruction and existing library practice. The programme was planned to enable students to acquire the ability to use the library and its information resources. Consideration of the most suitable methods for teaching led to the question, 'Is this what the students need to know?' with regard to existing practices. This sometimes led to modification in existing library practices and these will be described below.

When the text for the *Guide to the use of Chalmers Library* was being drawn up it was necessary to describe conditions of borrowing (*how* to obtain material) and the services available (*what* was there to be used). The actual text to use was the subject of considerable discussion. A prototype was drawn up and presented to the heads of the various library departments for their opinion and views. In the resulting discussions it was realised that some of the existing library practices were not really in agreement with the aims of the library as expressed in chapter two. Thus with regard to the borrowing regulations, the existing regulations stated that borrowers had to have some form of guarantor, either collectively through an organisation, such as the student union, or individually—through a person registered in the Gothenburg telephone directory. The library staff were all agreed that this system was, in practice, clumsy, and that it could not be said to 'actively stimulate the use' (general aim two) of the material held in by the library. Furthermore the regulations were not particularly helpful for the recovering of lost material. So the rules for borrowing were changed in order to make borrowing easier and stimulate the use of the collections. Thus it was decided that students from Chalmers could borrow by showing their student legitimation and other borrowers had to show an official identity card. (The vast majority of Swedish citizens possess these cards.) For people who did not have either of these means of identification—a very small number—the special regulations were retained. In the *Guide*, it was stated that Chalmers Library can be used by *all* who wish to make use of its services. This is in marked contrast to the negative impression created by rules and regulations about who may borrow and who may not. Similarly instead of saying that 'Reference books may not be removed from the library', it was said that 'Reference books are always available in the reading room.'

Another example of modification of library practice was in the treatment of the reserve book collection. Previously there had often only been one copy of some of the set books and students who had come to the library to look up some point had sometimes found that there was no copy available for reference. In connection with the description of this service it was decided to buy an extra copy of this type of set literature, so that there was always one copy available for reference, and the other copy could be borrowed for home reading. In this way a modification was made in the acquisition policy. Thus the planning phase of a programme of user orientation and instruction had affected the lending activities and acquisition policy.

Changes in library practice arising as a result of a programme of user education

One of the effects of the programme of user education at Chalmers has been to increase the contact between the students and academic staff and the library staff. This increased contact has led to increased awareness of the needs of the users, for example with regard to accessibility of material and acquisition of new material. This, in turn, has resulted in suggestions for changes in library practice.

Accessibility

Accessibility of information stored in the library depends partly on knowledge of what to look for and how to obtain it (provided by education of the library user) and the physical accessibility of the material—open or closed collections of literature, and the hours in which material is available.

During the courses on information retrieval it became more and more apparent that the students would have liked to have had free access to the information on open shelves. Chalmers University Library was built as a closed access library with literature stored in a book-tower to which the borrowers had no access. However, during 1976, reorganisation of the chemistry collection was carried out—the most recent material is now available on open-shelves in the Chemistry Library and the older material previously kept in closed-stacks has been made available on open shelves on the ground floor of the book-tower. Students follow a green line marked on the floor, from the Chemistry Library down two flights of stairs, through the post and packaging department, to the lowest floor of the book-tower. As this floor is unstaffed much work has been spent on the provision of signs for directing students to the material they require. In addition they can use the internal communication system to call for help from the main Chemistry Library. In spite of the inconvenience of the buildings—collections housed at considerable distance from each other—and the lack of staff in the book-tower, both students and staff from the chemistry departments have been very enthusiastic about this experiment.

As a result of the experiment with the chemistry collection it is hoped to extend the temporary opening of the book-tower, so that material is made available on open shelves for students from other schools of engineering. A start was made on this during the summer of 1977.

Opening the book-tower can only be regarded as a temporary solution to the problem of availability of material. The study conditions in the closed-tower environment are far from ideal, and plans have been drawn up for the extension of the library with an open and flexible building providing for the integration of open-shelved material and study places.

With the closed-access system students cannot go and take out the material that they wish to borrow themselves. They have to fill in a loan requisition form, and this is often regarded as being 'such a difficult business' as was seen in interviews with the students. At the present time it is not possible to obtain material after 16.15 hours as there are only two members of staff working during the evenings. (In practice, the evening staff have often taken out material for the students.) This means that students who finish their studies at 17.00 hours, cannot obtain literature until the next day. The closed collection is not available for use during the evenings. During the interviews students commented on this problem. At present a committee of the library staff has been formed to consider whether it would be possible to provide additional service during the evenings—to allow material to be taken out of the stacks and a limited amount of bibliographic help for library users. Should this be possible, it would increase the availability of the information by one third per year.

If periodical volumes and numbers can be borrowed it means that they are unavailable for other users. During the information retrieval courses it has been observed that students often come to a stop in their searches because material is out on loan. One way of getting round this problem is to increase the copying service and allow periodical articles to be obtained in the form of photocopies, rather than lending out recent numbers of periodicals. (The most recent material is that in highest demand.) This solution is being considered.

Facilities for the use of audio-visual media

As a result of the use of audio-visual material in user education programmes library staff became interested in the use of non-print media in education. Contact with the educational consultant and various members of the academic staff at Chalmers University showed that interesting experimental work making use of new media has been carried out during the last few years. For example, an audio-visual learning studio had been set up at the School of Civil Engineering. In this studio it was possible to combine the use of various media, and to present up to six tape/slide sequences in combination. These could be either teacher-controlled (via remote-control radio steering), automatic-controlled (via pre-pulses) or student-controlled (individual learning stations). Programmed instruction, making use of audio-visual material or computer terminals, was also available. At the School of Architecture a visualisation studio was opened in 1976, in which it was hoped to be able to present a three-dimensional overview of environments in which new buildings were planned. Use was made of the visualisation studio in the planning of the extension of the library. During the seventies there has been increasing attention given to the possibilities of language studies for engineers. A number of undergraduates choose an optional course in English studies. During this course extensive use is made of the language laboratory facilities possessed by the English department at Gothenburg University. This laboratory is, however, situated at some distance from Chalmers University.

These developments, together with experience gained from the tape/slide lending bank of library instruction material, have resulted in a growing realisation that the library must provide facilities for the use of audio-visual media and for the storage of such material as tape/slides, films, audio-tapes etc.

A start has been made, in the provision of facilities, by the construction of a well-equipped seminar room for thirty people. This room has a separate audio-visual unit where equipment for showing tape/slides, films and video-tapes is available. Simultaneous use of up to three units is possible. This seminar room was used for, amongst other things, the training of university teachers during 1976/77.

During the reorganisation of the material stored in the book-tower one area of the library, previously used for the storage of a number of periodicals—the gallery in the reading room—has been refitted. It is hoped to provide individual learning carrels where students will be able to listen to tapes (for language studies) or listen/watch audio-visual tape/slide presentations.

These examples show how the user education programme,with resultant increase in contact between the university teaching staff and the library, has indirectly affected library practice with regard to non-print media. The role of the library with regard to this type of material is closely dependent on its use within the education programme of the university. It is 'essential at the present time for librarians to be fully aware of the problems and possibilities of new media, and to examine them carefully in relation to the role and functions of each particular library' (Enright).

During talks with academic staff on the needs of the student users of the library it became apparent that many of them were unaware of the resources possessed by the library. This leads to duplication of resources and to non-use of material that costs a considerable sum of money. As a result of this, it was decided to start a project for the computer-based production of a list of the approximately 7000 periodicals held by the library. This could be used for the generation of a series of subject-orientated lists of holdings, for distribution to various departments of the university.

In addition studies are taking place as to the feasibility of reproducing the subject catalogue in micro-form for distribution to the university departments. With the advent of central cataloguing in the Swedish LIBRIS System (Library Information System), it will be possible to obtain micro-products of the material catalogued. Distribution of this information to the university departments could result in less duplication of material and consequent saving of the total resources of the university.

Improvement in library tools

In the user study carried out in connection with the planning of the programme of user education it was seen that many students did not use the subject catalogue, and many reported difficulties in its use. During the information searches carried out by students as part of their practical course in information retrieval, it was apparent that many had difficulty in finding appropriate search terms. Therefore, during the summer of 1975, a revision of the subject-index to the subject catalogue was carried out, in which the number of search terms was considerably increased, together with the cross-references.

The author catalogue had, previous to 1975, existed in one unbroken suite. However, the system for cataloguing had been changed in 1966. This combination of two systems in the same catalogue appeared to be confusing for the library users, in particular new users, so the author catalogue was split during the summer of 1974 into two parts, 'pre-1966' and '1966 onwards'. Signs explaining the use of these different systems were then put over the appropriate catalogues.

Improvement in library services

It was noted, in a survey of the daily use of the library carried out prior to the introduction of user education, that many users were unaware that the library had a reprocentre for photocopying. In 1974 there was a rather small notice placed inconspicuously amongst other notices on top of the circulation desk, giving directions to the reprocentre. This notice was replaced, during 1975, by a series of clearly lettered signs (in red) showing the way to the reprocentre from various parts of the library. This may have contributed to the fact that more people made use of the centre during 1975 than in 1974.

As a result of the course in information retrieval, more students needed to work in the main reference hall. Eighteen extra work places were provided by the reorganisation of the catalogues and rearrangement of other furniture.

Group rooms have been provided for students, on the second floor of the library, and the number of study places in the reading room has been increased by reorganising the reference gallery above the main study area.

Conclusion

One of the most important points arising from the study of the systematic development of a programme of user education at Chalmers University was that library user education is not an isolated function at the library. It needs on the one hand to be closely related to the needs of the users—that is to the general pattern of studies at the university; user education also needs to be closely integrated into other functions and activities of the library. It provides the opportunity for increased contact between members of the library staff and user groups such as students and members of the academic staff. This increased contact can lead to increased awareness of the need of the users. This, in turn, can lead to changes in other service functions of the library, in order to meet these needs. At Chalmers University Library the programme of user education has had a marked effect on many aspects of library work.

CHAPTER THIRTEEN

Resources and staffing

AN EFFECTIVE PROGRAMME of user education in whatever form is likely to raise user expectation in regard to the library. As far as possible that expectation must be matched in practice. Therefore before embarking on a formal programme it is necessary to ensure that everything possible has been done to make the library and its services appropriate, meaningful and helpful to the user. The manner and means by which this can be achieved have been alluded to several times in earlier chapters. In simple terms what is required is the provision of adequate resources and adequate exploitation of those resources.

In so far as is possible the library premises should be welcoming without being obtrusive; the physical environment provided by heating, lighting and noise level should be comfortable. Adequate seating and other furniture is necessary as is the provision of adequate teaching accommodation in the form of flexible seminar rooms. Whilst it is relatively easy to alter the physical provision within an existing building it is not possible at all to alter its physical location. There is an argument, considering user education alone, that in the planning of new library accommodation thought should be given to the provision of several smaller library units rather than one large central library. User education is usually most effective when librarian and user are in more constant and personal contact, a situation often found in smaller or departmental libraries. The librarian in such a situation is normally more available to help. However the disadvantages of costly duplication of materials, the manpower-intensive nature of the operation, and the more complex communications system required to coordinate several small libraries militate against the acceptance of such a proposal.

The major resource of any library is its stock. This not only must be adequate to meet the needs placed upon it, for example the provision of multiple copies of material in heavy demand, but must also be readily accessible physically by the convenient arrangement of documents on open access. Access in the physical sense must also be supported by access through other methods of exploitation of the stock. Mention has been made before of the necessity to provide a readily usable catalogue. Other processes and technical services should also be orientated to user needs and streamlined whilst retaining their efficiency. Prominent among these services are borrowing facilities and opening hours. A more efficient organisation of 'behind the scenes' operations could possibly lead to the involvement of more library staff in the 'front of house' interaction with users.

Mention has been made several times of the necessity for adequate guiding of the library building both in creating an atmosphere and as a means of exploiting the library's resources. Such guiding should provide a readily perceptible layout and directions for finding physical locations including instructions for the use of particular services. Comparisons are often made of the self-service nature of an open access library and the supermarket or department store. In the latter customers usually find what they require without formal guidance. Libraries may have a lot to learn from such shops where products are clearly displayed, where the layout is supported by adequate guiding, where staff provide courteous attention and generally appear helpful and informed. Users can browse and are helped to help themselves in finding what they require. As Heathcote notes 'their potential is not necessarily related to frantic attempts to be fashionable and trendy but to the substance of the goods and services they provide.'

Many methods of guiding have been adopted for use in libraries. The basic principles are essentially the same. According to Pollet these are, firstly, that signs must be placed so that they are easily locatable from entrances and major traffic flows and so placed that users will not feel self-conscious about pausing to read them. They should be of a hierarchical nature, those at the entrance being broad and total in their view of the library and those located in areas of divisions of the library containing comprehensive information about the particular location. Notices should be brief, with descriptions and procedures stated in the most concise manner possible, and properly edited. Finally they should be consistent in appearance and placement in relation to an imaginary horizon. Guiding is only one of the areas where graphic design opportunities are afforded to libraries. Stationery, publications, posters, exhibitions etc all are opportunities for the library to produce a coordinated design leading, hopefully, to a positive and recognisable image.

Library guides, while they cannot supplant adequate information provided at a point of need, are another way of enabling the user to find his own way in a library. They, too, require careful design planning to maximise their impact. Whilst there may be members of the library staff with the flair and imagination for this work it is essential that the library should combine its own professional expertise with those of other professionals in the design and production of guiding, guides, publications, teaching material etc. An editorial in *Infuse* sees the appointment

151

of graphic artists to the staff of Sheffield City Polytechnic Library and to the team of the Travelling Workshops Experiment at Newcastle Polytechnic (it should be noted that the University of York has used a professional graphic designer for some years) as a sign that there could at last be a proper appreciation of the fact that graphic design is too important an aspect of library operations to be left to amateurs. Other areas where professional help could be sought in the more effective presentation of matters pertinent to user education include photographic and audio-visual production and presentation, and also printing, particularly for posters, stationery, guides and other publications.

Guides and general publications are provided to make users or potential users aware of exactly what a library is and what services it can provide. They are important because the individual user and certainly the non-user may have little contact with the library staff. Printed material, properly designed and produced, will be noticed and will shape attitudes towards the library. In addition the tone and style of such publications, particularly if they concentrate on negative aspects such as regulations and rules, can also condition behaviour in libraries. Production of guides is but one form of publicity aimed at the creation of an image and an atmosphere within which a user education programme is more likely to be effective. Publicity itself is only one part of the broader programme of public relations or outreach. This programme is, as Taylor puts it, not orientation of the user to the library but orientation of the library to the user. Such a programme can only be successful if it is backed up by the provision of an efficient library service. It should also be noted that for an effective public relations exercise with regard to users and potential users it is necessary that the library has good public relations in-house. This will be discussed later as attitudes of librarians are considered.

In the provision of support services, publications, guiding, user education programmes, external professional expertise etc, finance is obviously a key resource. There are those who would claim that all the problems of user education could be solved if only the financial resources were available to implement the solution. However even sufficient finance is no guarantee of the effective implementation of a user education programme without the major resource required for such a programme the library staff in its totality.

Whether an idealised programme such as that described in chapter one would ever be attempted depends very much on the priorities of the chief librarian. Although the belief in the value of user education is widespread amongst such people it is often rated low in a list of the library's functions. User education and courses of instruction are still seen as a fringe activity low down on a list of priorities. The conservative tradition of many chief librarians leads them to feel that their job is to build up collections, organise them and offer help only when asked for it. The development and organisation of collections is a laudable aim but library services are now moving in a more positive direction. The only justification for employing high level staff is to employ them on high level activities which does not include cataloguing and accessioning books. As Taylor notes, too much emphasis is put on what comes in at the back door and too little attention is given to who comes in at the front door. If chief librarians really believe in the value of user education they must not only consider orientating the library to the user but also rebalancing their priorities to provide staff and time to do the job. They must also be prepared for the fact that effective user education pro- grammes do not lead to a decrease in the pressure on the library's services, rather, use becomes more sophisticated. Lack of observable benefits to the library may lead some librarians to consider whether such programmes have a cost/benefit relationship. This is unfortunate because if the need for user education is indisputable then it should not need to be subjected to cost/benefit analysis from the library's point of view.

How senior librarians organise their staff, whether it be along subject specialist or functional lines, appears to have little bearing on the impact of user education programmes. The definition of the two types has, in any event, now become so blurred that a continuum exists in job des- criptions between the traditional definitions of the two roles. Not only do tutor-librarians for whom the functional role is more easily defined meet with success but so do some subject specialists in the teaching/ advisory element of their role. What is important is not how the librarian is described but how the emphasis is placed in the organisation of the work of the library staff to provide a high priority for communication with users. Some subject specialists however are noticeably less enthus- iastic about the teaching component of their job, whereas librarians with the functional role of user education are quite naturally slightly more committed.

This leads naturally on to a discussion of the necessary qualities, qualifications and attitudes for those engaged in user education, since these are more important than organisational considerations. There are two schools of thought about qualities and qualifications required. One suggests the priority should be good subject qualifications (enabling the librarian to be regarded favourably by his academic colleagues and enabling him to relate user education to the subject field in a more relevant manner) followed by professional qualifications in librarianship. After this teaching experience and personal qualities would be rated equally. The other school of thought suggests that personal qualities are more important than qualifications, though the latter cannot be ignored. Desirable personal qualities are thought to be enthusiasm, an ability to communicate clearly and effectively, public relations ability, friendliness, patience, humility and maturity. This latter quality argues for a person with experience, though there are those who would argue that it would be easier for the student to identify with a younger person.

Bound up with the whole question of personal qualities is that of attitudes. Enthusiasm was noted as the most important quality in the list above of desirable qualities. It is also an attitude of mind which requires a strong motivation on the part of the librarian for it to be conveyed to the user. The librarian needs to be self-motivated, that is, he must want to do the teaching/advisory work and not do it because he has to. The librarian's attitude to the job and to the user may well require modification, if Urquhart is correct. He believes that substantial progress can only be achieved if the library world accepts the idea that its job is not to answer questions for users but to show them how to answer the questions for themselves. This is a theme taken up by his successor Line who compares the attitude of the person involved in user education with that of a driving instructor. Information handling, like learning to drive a car, is a skill that has to be developed by learning it beside someone who is better at it then you but is not going to be patronising about it. Each user must therefore be seen as an individual, which bears out Hackman's prediction noted earlier that the revolution in user education will be less concerned with new methods and more with a realistic and empathetic relationship between the librarian and user and a clearer perception of their mutual purpose. Creation of positive attitudes of this kind will of necessity lead on to an improved image of the librarian.

Library staff attitudes (and behaviour) to users is as important as the student's attitudes to the library staff. Positive attitudes and positive approaches towards users and user education need creating. Not only is there a need for a positive approach to users but also a need for librarians to make themselves approachable. Regular personal contact is necessary in the provision of an effective user education programme. Approachability is a function of motivation and a willingness to go beyond the physical boundaries of the library into the community it serves. User education programmes with the most impact are those where librarians are active members of the institution or community they serve. Improvements in librarian/user personal contacts are possible by the provision of training even though the key to their success is motivation.

Unfortunately many librarians feel ill-prepared by their librarianship training for the tasks of user education and many engaged in teaching the use of library resources are conscious of the fact that they have had no formal training in teaching or learning methods. Most are not skilled in educational techniques and the communication skills required for group interactions or person to person contact. Such skills and techniques appear not to be acquired in library school training. Library schools though are providing newly qualified librarians, orientated to user services, motivated towards user education and with positive attitudes to service. However the lack of training in basic skills and techniques required for user education results in an inability to set realistic aims and objectives for programmes and the fact that some librarians are apt to be content conscious (ie they teach what they know) rather than method conscious (ie teaching ways of finding out). This approach to the literature of a subject with a bibliographic approach is not surprising because this is how they themselves were taught. In library school the approach may be valid but it is not usually relevant to the average library user. Library instruction is peculiarly difficult to make interesting at the best of times; to do it without training makes it even more so.

Some remedial work can be done by means of in-service training programmes, by attendance at local courses organised for new teachers in polytechnics and universities, or by post-experience seminars. It would be better however if the trainee librarian were enabled to acquire some basic skills for user education at the same time as he was learning other basic professional skills. Such basic skills could be supplemented later both by experience and by post-experience courses.

What are the elements that might go to make up a programme of basic training? It is quite clear that what a course should not be is an audio-visual production course. It should be as practical a course as possible giving students opportunities to learn by doing. User education must be considered in its widest context (see, for example chapter one). It should not be considered only in the context of academic libraries but libraries in general, some of the most exciting opportunities for user education being found in public and special libraries. It should include interaction with non-users as well as users. The philosophy, history and study of present practice would form an introduction to be followed by consideration of user needs and the conduct of user studies. It is necessary to learn the techniques of determining what these needs actually are as opposed to what the librarian perceives them to be. Comparison of the results of user studies for different library user groups would be instructive and could lead on to a consideration of what the aims and objectives of a programme of user education and outreach might be for the different user groups. These would be affected by the different target groups and would vary in their affective situations of the cognitive balance. Analysis of a problem in this way must lead on to the synthesis of a solution. The effect of different types and levels of objectives on the teaching/learning methods of implementation of the solution and the aids to this communication would naturally include consideration of the different techniques and aids that can be employed. Practice in the use of these techniques (which would include audio-visual presentations) should be given but in the context of choice of medium and technique to meet specified objectives. This would demonstrate how methods used are affected by different statements of aims, objectives and target populations.

In considering situations involving non-users particularly, it will be necessary to include elements of publicity and public relations work. Displays, exhibitions, involvement in the community, the use of local radio and other communications media could all be included. Techniques of effective writing (particularly for guides) and effective speaking could be linked with effective listening to produce in summary an element of the course which could be labelled effective communication. Barriers to communication in the library situation should be considered before looking at factors affecting, and the methods for improving, interpersonal communication or group dynamics. Discussion could focus here on the role of an advisory service as compared with a reference service; and study, together with practical work, could be made of techniques involved in exploiting person-to-person communication. For example approachability is involved in establishing a climate for communication. Effective listening is involved in the stage of problem/question negotiation—in order to elucidate the need of the other person. How can the librarian help the user to structure his question from a nebulous feeling? Finally there is the actual provision of the help where an element of effective speaking is involved.

Counselling skills as well as communication skills can of course be required in such situations. It is not only necessary to acquire these skills but to practise them. In practice it often appears that people with these qualities are born not made. The same natural ability can often be seen in practical teaching situations where knowledge or ideas must be imparted in a meaningful, clear and relevant manner. However such skills and teaching ability can be developed by sympathetic training. Students at library school should in the course of their one, two or three years there experience all types of teaching/learning situation. Out of this experience it should be possible to consider the usefulness of each method and its applicability in given situations of user education. Here again meaningful practice is essential. The trend in higher education towards self-instruction and private study requiring the greater use of libraries would be considered here and should be linked with the effect of this trend on the whole of the library service and not just its implications for user education. Undoubtedly there are many other elements that merit consideration for inclusion in a basic programme to enable librarians to become more actively involved in user education. However no matter how much practical work is included in the basic course there is no substitute for experience and it may be better to provide further training in the provision of appropriate post-experience courses, for example ones dealing with evaluation techniques or methodology of educational research.

Of course it is not just the professional staff who require training. Very often the junior staff are the first contact the user has with the library and they can contribute significantly to the creation of an image of the library and an atmosphere in which users can seek help. Attitudes of junior staff are very often copied from those of their senior colleagues who should therefore lead by example. Provision of forms of in-service training for junior staff though can contribute to their more effective communication with users and this aspect of the role of senior staff, the training element, should not be lost sight of in the basic course outlined above.

Finally the last resource to be mentioned but arguably one of the more important in user education is the teacher. The concept of integration and the role of the academic was discussed briefly in chapter one. Although a lot of valuable user education is possible without the support of the academic, particularly in individual instruction, it has been the case that treating user education as a separate entity, divorced from the involvement of the teacher, has not been successful. The teacher is a resource to be used, if user education is to create an environment in which information-handling appropriate to a particular level of education is to be learned at that level. Only then will it form a natural part of the student's education.

Selected references

Andersen, L 'Training in the use of libraries' in Library Association of Australia 14th Biennial Conference, Brisbane, 1967 *Changing concepts of librarianship* Proceedings of the conference. Brisbane, LAA Conference Committee, 1968. Volume I, pp 13-25.

Astin, A W and Panos, R J 'The evaluation of educational programs' in Thorndike, R L (ed) *Educational measurement* 2nd ed. Washington, American Council of Education, 1971, pp 733-51.

Axeen, M E 'Teaching the use of the library to undergraduates: an experimental comparison of computer based instruction and the conventional lecture method' (AD 657216).

Beeler, R J (ed) *Evaluating library use instruction* Ann Arbor, Pierian Press, 1975.

Bloom, B S (ed) *Taxonomy of educational objectives. Handbook I: The cognitive domain*. New York, McKay, 1956.

Bloom, B S et al *Handbook on formative and summative evaluation of student learning*. New York, McGraw Hill, 1971.

Bloomfield, M 'Testing for library-use competence' in Lubans, J (ed) *Educating the library user* London, Bowker, 1974, pp 221-31.

Bolner, M *Planning and developing a library orientation program* Ann Arbor, Pierian Press, 1975.

Bonn, G S 'Training laymen in the use of the library' in *The state of the library art 2* (1) New Brunswick, Rutgers University Press, 1960.

Bradfield, V J et al 'Librarians or academics? User education at Leicester Polytechnic' *Aslib proceedings 29* (3), 1977, pp 133-42.

Brittain, M and Irving, A *Trends in the education of users of libraries and information services in the USA* BLRD Report 5297, 1976.

Butterfield, M B 'Project LOEX means library orientation exchange' *RQ 13* (1), 1973, pp 39-42.

Carey, R J P *Library guiding: a systems approach to exploitation* London, Bingley, 1974; Hamden, Conn, Linnet.

Childs, C E N 'Do students have to use libraries?' *Times higher education supplement* 1 June 1973, p 24.

Christiansen, M S *Bibliografiske hjaelpemidler til det botaniske studium* (Bibliographical aids for botanical studies). Copenhagen, Botanisk Centralbibliotek, 1971.

Clark, A S 'Computer-assisted library instruction' in Lubans, J (ed) *Educating the library user* London, Bowker, 1974, pp 336-49.

Clod Poulsen, S *Litteratustrudier som led i paedagogisk-psykologisk forskning* Copenhagen, Danmarks Paedagogoske Institut (Publikation nr 78), 1975.

College and Research Libraries' News Part 3, 1977, 63; Part 4, 1977, 92; Part 5, 1977, 125; Part 6, 1977, 182; Part 7, 1977, 205.

Cowley, J (ed) *Libraries in higher education: the user approach to service* London, Bingley, 1975; Hamden, Conn, Linnet.

Crawford, C and Chun, M *Hawaii school libraries: a manual for organisation and services* Honolulu, State of Hawaii Department of Education, 1964.

Crossley, C A 'Tuition in the use of the library and the subject literature in the University of Bradford' *Journal of documentation 24* (2), 1968, pp 91-7.

Crossley, C A and Clews, J P Evaluation of the use of educational technology in information handling instruction: a literature review and bibliography submitted to the British Library Research and Development Department, 1974. (OSTI Report 5220)

Cuming, A 'The organisation of a university library' *Library Association record 28*, 1926, pp 129-37.

Deer, G H 'The Peabody Library information test: a study of its validity and reliability' *Journal of experimental education 9*, 1941, pp 233-36.

Dudley, M 'Teaching library skills to college students' *Advances in librarianship 3*, 1973, pp 83-105.

Dunn, W R et al 'Investigations of self-instructional materials in medical education' in Mann and Bronston (eds) *Aspects of educational technology III* London, Pitman, 1969.

Dyson, A J 'Organising undergraduate library instruction: the English and American experience' *Journal of academic librarianship 1* (1), 1975, pp 9-13.

Earnshaw, F 'An example of cooperative development of library use instruction programs' in Lubans, J (ed) *Educating the library user* London, Bowker, 1974.

The education of users of scientific and technical information Report from a workshop held at the University of Bath, 14-16 September 1973. Bath University Library, 1973.

Ellison, J W and Molenda, C 'Making yourself approachable' *New library world 77*, 1976, pp 214-5.

Enright, B J *New media and the library in education* London, Bingley, 1972; Hamden, Conn, Linnet.

Erkko, K *Teknillisen korkeakoulun kirjasston käyttoselivity* (Survey of the use of Helsinki University of Technology Library). Mimeograph 1970.

Feagley, E M et al *A library orientation test for college freshmen* New York, Columbia University, 1955.

Fjällbrant, N 'The use of tape/slide guides in library instruction' *Tidskrift för dokumentation 29* (5), 1973, pp 116-21, 125.

Fjällbrant, N and Westberg, S 'Forskningsbiblioteken utbildar sina nyttjare' (Research libraries train their users) *Biblioteksbladet 59* (1), 1974, pp 5-6.

Fjällbrant, N 'Library instruction for students in universities in Britain' *Chalmers University of Technology transactions 335*, 1974.

Fjällbrant, N and Westberg, S 'Library instruction in academic libraries in Sweden' *Chalmers University of Technology transactions 336*, 1974.

Fjällbrant, N 'User instruction in the libraries of the technological universities in Scandianvia: some recent developments' *IATUL proceedings 7* (2), December 1974, pp 54-9.

Fjällbrant, N 'The use of audiovisual material in library instruction' in *Ikke-boklig materiale i bibliotekene.* Foredrag ved NVBF's medlemsmøde i Trondheim 24-26 Juni 1974, Trondheim, 1975.

Fjällbrant, N and Westberg, S 'Forskningsbibliotekens roll för nya högskolan' (The role of research libraries in relation to the new higher education) *Biblioteksldadet 60* (15), 1975, pp 276, 278-80.

Fjällbrant, N 'A comparison of user instruction in Scandinavian and British academic libraries' *Chalmers University of Technology transactions 337*, 1975.

Fjällbrant, N 'Teaching methods for the education of the library user' *Libri 26* (4), 1976, pp 252-267.

Fjällbrant, N 'The development of a programme of user education at Chalmers University of Technology Library' PhD thesis, University of Surrey, 1976.

Fjällbrant, N 'A study of user behaviour and needs at the biomedical section of Gothenburg University Library' *CTHB Publikation II*, Gothenburg, 1976.

Fjällbrant, N 'User education programmes in Swedish academic libraries. A study of developments in the years 1973-77' *CTHB Publikation 14*, Gothenburg, 1977.

Ford, G 'Research in user behaviour in university libraries' *Journal of documentation 29* (1), 1973, pp 85-106.

Fox, P *Reader instruction methods in academic libraries, 1973* Cambridge, The University Library, 1974.

Gardner, J J 'Point-of-use library instruction' *Drexel Library quarterly 8* (3), 1972, pp 281-5.

Genung, H 'Can machines teach the use of the library?' *College and research libraries 28* (1), 1967, pp 25-30.

Givens, J 'The use of resources in the learning experience' *Advances in librarianship 4*, 1974, pp 149-74.

Gjersvik, R 'Brukeropplaering ved NTHS bibliotek' (User instruction at the University of Technology Library, Trondheim) *UNIT, NTH, Biblioteket, Rapport 12* Trondheim, BTH-Trykk, 1972.

Gluchowicz, Z 'Selective dissemination of information: a transdisciplinary information retrieval system at the Royal Institute of Technology, Stockholm' *IAG journal 4*, 1971, pp 131.

Griffin, L W and Clarke, J A 'Orientation and instruction of graduate students in the use of the university library: a survey' *College and research libraries 33* (6), 1972, pp 467-72.

Gross, N et al *Implementing organizational innovations* New York, Harper and Row, 1971.

Guidelines for library handbooks Washington, Federal Library Committee, 1972.

Haaland, G 'Library instruction in Norway' Proceedings of the NVBF Anglo-Scandinavian Seminar on library user education, November 2-4 1976, Gothenburg, Sweden. *CTHB Publikation 12*, Gothenburg, 1977.

Hackman, M 'Proposal for a program of library instruction' *Drexel Library quarterly 7* (3/4), 1971, pp 299-308.

Hansen, L N 'Computer assisted instruction in library use: an evaluation' *Drexel Library quarterly 8* (3), 1972, pp 345-55.

Harlan, R 'Welcoming notes' in *Instruction in the use of the college and university library* Berkeley, University of California School of Librarianship, 1970.

Harris, C 'Illuminative evaluation of user education programmes' *Aslib proceedings 29* (10), 1977, pp 348-62.

Hatt, F 'My kind of library tutoring' *Library Association record 70*, 1968, pp 258-61.

Heathcote, D 'Public relations and publicity' in Cowley, J (ed) *Libraries in higher education: the user approach to service* London, Bingley, 1975; Hamden, Conn, Linnet; pp 39-64.

Henning, P A and Stillman, M E (eds) 'Integrating library instruction in the college curriculum' *Drexel Library quarterly 7* (3/4), 1971.

161

Henning, P A and Shapiro, J (eds) 'Library instruction: methods, materials, evaluation' *Drexel Library quarterly 8* (3), 1972.

Hernon, P 'Library lectures and their evaluation: a survey' *Journal of academic librarianship 1* (3), 1975, pp 14-8.

Hills, P J 'Library instruction and the development of the individual' *Journal of librarianship 6* (4), 1974, pp 255-63.

Hills, P J 'An investigation of some applications of self-teaching systems in the University of Surrey' PhD thesis, University of Surrey, 1974.

Horton, J J 'Library liaison with social scientists: relationships in a university context' *Aslib proceedings 29* (4), 1977, pp 146-57.

Howe, J A M and Delamont, S 'Towards an evaluation strategy for CAI projects' *Bionics research reports 15*, 1974. (School of Artificial Intelligence, University of Edinburgh).

Husén, T (ed) *International study of achievement in mathematics* New York, Wiley, 1967.

Hutton, R S 'Instruction in library use: a needed addition to the university curriculum' Report of the proceedings of the seventeenth annual conference of Aslib, 1942, pp 27-30.

Ingwersen, P et al 'A study of the user-librarian negotiation process' in *EURIM II*. A European conference on the applications of research in information services and libraries. London, Aslib, 1977, p 203.

Intergovernmental conference on the planning of national documentation, library and archives infrastructures, Paris 23-27 September 1974. *Final report*, Paris, Unesco, 1975.

Jørgensen, B et al (eds) *Introduktion til historie* Copenhagen, Akademisk Forlag, 1970.

Jørgensen, F 'DTB's undervisning i udnyttelse af den tekniske litteratur' (The National Technological Library of Denmark's instruction in the use of scientific literature) in *Danmarks Tekniske Bibliotek med Dansk Central för Dokumentation* 25 ar. Copenhagen, 1967.

Jørgensen, F 'User education at the National Technological Library of Denmark' (to be published in *IATUL proceedings 9*, 1977).

Jolley, L 'The function of the university library' *Journal of documentation 18*, 1962, pp 133-42.

Jones, D E 'Information resources for the social sciences: a library seminar for university teaching and research staff' *Education libraries bulletin 47*, summer 1974, pp 27-35.

Kennedy, J R et al 'Course-related library instruction: a case-study of the English and biology departments at Earlham College' *Drexel Library quarterly 7* (3/4), 1971, pp 277-97.

Kibbey, R A and Weiner, A M 'USF library lectures revisited' *RQ 13* (2), 1973, pp 139-42.

Kirk, T G 'A comparison of two methods of library instruction for students in introductory biology' *College and research libraries 32* (6), 1971, pp 465-74.

Kirk, T G and Lynch, M J 'Bibliographic instruction in academic libraries: new developments' *Drexel Library quarterly 8* (3), 1972, pp 357-65.

Kivelä, T 'Erfarenheter fran videobandning och TV-undervisning av användare vid tekniska högskolans i Helsingfors bibliotek' (Experience of video and TV instruction of users at the Helsinki University of Technology Library). Paper presented at NORDDOK's Scandinavian symposium on user instruction, Oslo, 1974.

Knapp, P B *The Monteith College library experiment* New York, Scarecrow Press, 1964.

Krathwohl, D R et al *Taxonomy of educational objectives. Handbook II: The affective domain*. New York, McKay, 1964.

Kuo, F F 'A comparison of six versions of science library instruction' *College and research libraries 34* (4), 1973, pp 287-90.

Kvam, B L 'Library instruction in Norway' Proceedings of the NVBF Anglo-Scandinavian seminar on library user education, November 2-4 1976, Gothenburg, Sweden. *CTHB Publikation 12*, Gothenburg, 1977.

Lau, B 'Library instruction in Denmark' Proceedings of the NVBF Anglo-Scandinavian seminar on library user education, November 2-4 1976, Gothenburg, Sweden. *CTHB Publikation 12*, Gothenburg, 1977.

Lee, S H (ed) *Library orientation* Ann Arbor, Pierian Press, 1972.

Lee, S H (ed) *A challenge for academic libraries* Ann Arbor, Pierian Press, 1973.

Library Association, University and Research Section. Working party on instruction in the use of libraries and in bibliography at the universities *Library Association record 51*, 1949, pp 149-50.

Lindberg, A 'Teaching library users at Linköping University Library' (To be published in *IATUL proceedings 9*, 1977).

Line, M B and Tidmarsh, M 'Student attitudes to the university library: a second survey at Southhampton University' *Journal of documentation 22* (2), 1966, pp 123-35.

Line, M B 'Information services in academic libraries' in Lincoln, C M (ed) *Educating the library user* Loughborough, University of Technology Library, 1970.

Line, M B 'The case for information officers' in Lubans, J (ed) *Educating the library user* London, Bowker, 1974.

Line, M B 'The prospect before us' *School librarian 24* 1976, pp 5-13.

Ljungars, K 'Experience from a postgraduate course in library techniques and information retrieval at the Karolinska Institut' *KIB Rapport 4* Stockholm, 1974.

LOEX news 4 (1), 1977, pp 1-2.

Lubans, J 'Non-use of an academic library' *College and research libraries* 32, 1971, 364-7.

Lubans, J 'Evaluating library-user education programs' *Drexel Library quarterly 8* (3), 1972, pp 325-43.

Lubans, J (ed) *Educating the library user* London, Bowker, 1974.

Lubans, J 'Objectives for library use instruction in educational curricula' in Lubans, J (ed) *Educating the library user* London, Bowker, 1974, pp 211-20.

Lubans, J 'Evaluating library user education programs' in Lubans, J (ed) *Educating the library user* London, Bowker, 1974, pp 232-53.

McCoy, R E 'Automation in freshman library instruction' *Wilson Library bulletin 36*, 1962, pp 468-70, 472.

Mackenzie, A G 'Reader instruction in modern universities' *Aslib proceedings 21* (7), 1969, pp 271-79.

McLeish, J *The lecture method* Cambridge, Institute of Education, 1968.

Mann, P H 'Communication about books to undergraduates' *Aslib proceedings 26* (6), 1974, pp 250-6.

Markland, K 'Library instruction into technical education at the University of Lulea' (To be published in *IATUL proceedings 9*, 1977).

Martyn, J 'The OSTI university information officers project' in Ayres, F and Hall, J (eds) *Information services in university libraries* London, SCONUL, 1974, pp 46-54.

Melum, V V 1971 survey of library orientation and instruction programs *Drexel Library quarterly 7* (3/4), pp 225-53.

Melum, V V 'Library orientation in the college and university' *Wilson Library bulletin 46* (1), 1971, pp 59-66.

Mews, H 'Library instruction concerns people' *Library Association record 72* (1), 1970, pp 8-10.

Mews, H *Reader instruction in colleges and universities: an introductory handbook* London, Bingley, 1972; Hamden, Conn, Linnet.

Mews, H 'Teaching th use of books and libraries, with particular reference to academic libraries' in Whatley, H A (ed) *British librarianship and information science 1966-1970* London, The Library Association, 1972, pp 601-9.

Millis, C 'Involving students in library orientation projects: a commitment to help' in Lee, S H (ed) *A challenge for academic libraries* Ann Arbor, Pierian Press, 1973, pp 63-98.

Mirwis, A 'Academic library instruction—a bibliography 1960-1970' *Drexel Library quarterly 7* (3/4), 1971, pp 327-35.

Moghdam, D 'User training for on-line information retrieval systems' *Journal of the American Society for Information Science 26*, 1975, pp 184-8.

Nettlefold, B A 'A course in communication and information retrieval for undergraduate biologists' *Journal of biological education 9* (5), 1975, pp 201-5.

Nielsen, E K 'On the teaching of subject bibliography in history' *Libri 24*, 1974, pp 171-208.

Öberg, I L 'Use of videotape material in library instruction' Proceedings of the NVBF Anglo-Scandinavian seminar on library user education, November 2-4, 1976. Gothenburg, Sweden. *CTHB-Publikation 12*, Gothenburg, 1977.

Oklahoma Curriculum Improvement Commission, Library Resources Division and the State Library Service Committee. Curriculum Guide for the teaching of library skills: grades K-12. Oklahoma State Department of Education, 1969.

Olving, S 'Education of graduate engineers in Sweden' *European journal of engineering education 2*, 1977, pp 109-14.

Parlett, M and Hamilton, D *Evaluation as illumination: a new approach to the study of innovatory programmes.* Centre for Research in the Behavioural Sciences, University of Edinburgh, Edinburgh, 1972.

Perkins, F L *A determination of the correlation between the Peabody and Bennett tests* Denver, University of Denver, 1964.

Pollet, D 'You can get there from here: new directions in library signage' *Wilson Library bulletin 50* (6), 1976, pp 456-62.

Pugh, L C 'Library instruction programmes for undergraduates: historical development and current practice' *Library world 71*, 1970, pp 267-73.

Rader, H B 'Bibliography on library orientation 1973, 1974, 1975' *Reference services review 2* Jan/March 1974, 91-3; *3* Jan/March 1975, 29-31; *4*, Oct/Dec 1976, 91-3.

Rader, H B (ed) *Academic library instruction: objectives, programs and faculty involvement* Ann Arbor, Pierian Press, 1975.

Rader, H B (ed) *Faculty involvement in library instruction* Ann Arbor, Pierian Press, 1976.

Rader, H B (ed) *Library instruction in the seventies: state of the art* Ann Arbor, Pierian Press, 1977.

Readers' Advisory Service, University of Sussex. 'Sixth form library visits.' *Library Association record 77* (4), 1975, pp 79-81.

Reid, B J 'Bibliographic teaching in French and politics at the University of Leicester' *Journal of librarianship 5* (4), 1973, pp 293-303.

Revill, D H 'Teaching methods in the library: a survey from the educational point of view' *Library world 71*, 1970, pp 243-8.

Rhodes, R G and Evans, A J 'The educational role of the university library and the provision of information services' *IATUL proceedings 7* (1), 1978, pp 11-25.

Rigg, R P *Audiovisual aids and techniques* London, Hamish Hamilton, 1969.

Roy, B *The needs of the student library user as seen by academic staff, library staff, and students* Report of a pilot study at the University of Surrey. Guildford, Institute for Educational Technology, University of Surrey, 1974.

Sabsay, P 'An attempt at integrating education in information retrieval into university studies' Paper presented at 1976 EUSIDIC Conference December 1-3 1976, Graz.

Scriven, M 'The methodology of evaluation' in Tyler, R W et al *Perspectives of curriculum evaluation* Chicago, Rand McNally, 1967, pp 39-83.

Scrivener, J E 'Instruction in library use: the persisting problem' *Australian academic and research libraries 3* (2), 1972, pp 87-119.

Shores, L 'The college becomes a library' *Drexel Library quarterly 4* (1), 1968, pp 31-44.

Shores, L and Moore, J E *Peabody library information test* Minneapolis, Educational Test Bureau, Educ Publ, 1940.

Some facts about Chalmers University of Technology, Gothenburg Chalmers Tekniske Högskola, 1976.

Stake, R E 'The countenance of educational evaluation' *Teachers college record 68* (7), 1967, pp 523-40.

Stake, R E 'Program evaluation, particularly responsive evaluation' *Reports from the Institute of Education, University of Gothenburg 35*, Gothenburg, 1974.

Stevens, C H et al 'Library Pathfinders: a new possibility for cooperative reference service' *College and research libraries 34* (1), 1973, pp 40-6.

Stevens, C H and Gardner, J J 'Point of use library instruction' in Lubans, J (ed) *Educating the library user* London, Bowker, 1974.

Stevenson, M B *Problems and evaluation of reader instruction in British university libraries* MA thesis, University College, London, 1973.

Stevenson, M B 'Education in the use of information in university and academic environments' *Aslib proceedings 28* (1), 1976, pp 17-21.

Stevenson, M B 'Libraries and users: problems of communication' Proceedings of the NVBF Anglo-Scandinavian seminar on library user education, November 2-4 1976, Gothenburg, Sweden. *CTHB-Publikation 12*, Gothenburg, 1977.

Stevenson, M B *User education programmes: a study of their development, organisation, methods and assessment* BLRD Report 5320. Wetherby, British Library, 1977.

Stevenson, M B 'Education of users of libraries and information services' *Journal of documentation 33* (1), 1977, pp 53-78.

Taylor, R S 'Orienting the library to the user' in *Use, mis-use and non-use of academic libraries* New York, New York Library Association College and University Libraries Section, 1970.

Taylor, R S 'Orienting the library to the user at Hampshire College *Drexel Library quarterly 7* (3/4), 1971 pp 351-64.

Thornton, J L 'Too few libraries are organised for readers' *Library Association record 78* (6), 1976, pp 255-6, 258.

Tidmarsh, M 'Instruction in the use of academic libraries' in Saunders, W L (ed) *University and research library studies* Oxford, Pergamon, 1968.

Timmermann, P *Betragtninger over søgestrategi* (Thoughts on information search techniques) Copenhagen, Danmarks Biblioteksskole, 1976.

Tornudd, E *Selvitys opiskelijoiden suhtautumisesta Helsingin teknillisen koreakoulun kirjstoon* (Survey into student attitudes to the library) Occasional Paper 10 Helsinki University of Technology Library, 1973.

'Towards guidelines for bibliographic instruction in academic libraries' *College and research libraries news 36*, May 1975, pp 137-9, 169-71.

University of Colorado Libraries, Library Use Instruction Committee *Draft objectives in the University of Colorado libraries provision of instruction in the use of libraries* Boulder, University of Colorado Libraries, 1973.

Urquhart, D J 'Developing user independence' *Aslib proceedings 18* (12), 1966, pp 351-6.

Uuttu, L-K 'Experience of library instruction in Finland—with a case study from Helsinki University of Technology' Proceedings of the NVBF Anglo-Scandinavian seminar on library user education, November 2-4 1976, Gothenburg, Sweden. *CTHB-Publikation 12*, Gothenburg, 1977.

'Vejledning af studerende i praktisk biblioteksbenyttelse og fagbibliografi' (Instruction of students in the practical use of libraries and in subject bibliography) Rapport fra møde pa Statsbiblioteket i Aarhus 19 November 1970. *Sammenslutningen af Danmarks Forskningsbiblioteker Publikation 2.*

Vernon, K D C 'Introducing users to sources of information: the approach of the London Business School' *Aslib proceedings 27* (11/12), 1975, pp 468-73.

Vogel, J T 'Critical overview of the evaluation of library instruction' *Drexel Library quarterly 8* (3), 1972, pp 315-23.

Watkins, D R 'Some notes on orienting the library to the user' in *Use, mis-use and non-use of academic libraries* New York, New York Library Association College and University Libraries Section, 1970.

Wiggins, M E 'The development of library use instructional programs' *College and research libraries 33* (6), 1972 pp 473-9.

Wiggins, M E and Low, D S 'Use of an instructional psychology model for development of library use instructional programs' *Drexel Library quarterly 8* (3), 1972, pp 269-79.

Will, L D 'Finding information: acourse for physics students' *Physics bulletin 23*, 1972, pp 539-40.

Wright, G H *The library in colleges of commerce and technology; a guide to the use of the library as an instrument of education* London, Deutsch, 1966.

INDEX

170